A Primer of ALGOL 60 Programming

A.P.I.C. Studies in Data Processing
No. 2

A Primer of
ALGOL 60
Programming

by
E. W. DIJKSTRA

Together with
Report on the Algorithmic Language ALGOL 60

Published for
THE AUTOMATIC PROGRAMMING INFORMATION CENTRE
Brighton College of Technology, England
by

1962
ACADEMIC PRESS
LONDON AND NEW YORK

ACADEMIC PRESS INC. (LONDON) LTD.
24/28 Oval Road
London, N.W. 1

U.S. Edition published by

ACADEMIC PRESS INC.

111 FIFTH AVENUE

NEW YORK, NEW YORK 10003

Library of Congress Catalog Card Number: 62-13885
SBN: 12 2162501 1

First Printing 1962
Second Printing, 1963
Third Printing, 1966
Fourth Printing, 1967
Fifth Printing, 1969
Sixth Printing 1973

Reprinted photolitho in Great Britain by Page Bros (Norwich) Ltd., Mile Cross
Lane, Norwich.

Foreword

This is the second of a series of studies in data processing to be issued, from time to time, for the Automatic Programming Information Centre, by the Academic Press. The series will, it is hoped, make available in convenient form material of interest to those concerned with the many problems of automatic programming whether in the field of commercial or scientific computing.

We are most grateful to the author and to the Mathematical Centre, Amsterdam, for their co-operation in making possible this English translation of Dr. Dijkstra's *'Programming Primer for ALGOL 60.'* For the convenience of the reader the text of the official *'Report on the Algorithmic Language ALGOL 60'* is reproduced as an appendix. Our thanks are also here expressed to Mr. M. Woodger, of the Mathematics Division of the National Physical Laboratory, one of the co-authors of the ALGOL 60 Report, for the great care with which he has read the proofs of both the Primer and the Report and for his never-failing assistance in many other ways to A.P.I.C.

RICHARD GOODMAN

Brighton College of Technology,
Brighton, England.

Preface

One aim the originators of ALGOL 60 had in mind was that ALGOL 60 should bring the enormous potentialities of modern automatic computing machines within the reach of a large group of potential users. This should include those users for whom an automatic computing machine is primarily a tool which they can use in order to obtain results of interest to them. In designing ALGOL 60 every effort has been made to ensure that this particular tool is the right one for the job.

It is intended that the language ALGOL 60 can be used for describing a computational process, independent of the particular machine that will be chosen for its actual execution. In order to ensure that two different computers would handle a given ALGOL program in a sufficiently similar manner, it was first of all necessary to fix the rules of ALGOL 60 precisely. This has already been done, and the rules are given in an unusual, but, for this purpose, necessarily unambiguous manner in the official ALGOL 60 report, '*Report on the Algorithmic Language Algol 60*' by J. W. Backus, *et al.** This report was never intended as a primer and anyone who tries to learn ALGOL 60 from it will find this rather difficult, unnecessarily difficult, I might say.

This book has been written in order to ease the problem of learning ALGOL 60. This has caused some duplication, albeit in other words, of the material in the official report. If this book should deviate from the implications of the official report, I should like to emphasize that the latter is the one to accept.

E. W. DIJKSTRA

* See Appendix

Author's Preface to the English Edition

In April 1961 the AUTOMATIC PROGRAMMING INFORMATION CENTRE, held at the Brighton College of Technology, a three-day school on 'ALGOL 60 Programming', at which the author was one of the tutors. On account of the enthusiasm shown by those attending the School and the apparent need for a readable introduction to ALGOL 60, the author was then asked to co-operate in the publication of an English version of his ALGOL 60 Manual, originally written in Dutch.

It is a course with special reference to the ALGOL 60 translator of the Mathematical Centre, which was in operation as early as August 1960. The special restrictions of this translator are very few in number; they are, however, clearly marked as such and it was judged a great asset that this Manual was part of a working system with which considerable experience had already been gained.

The author wishes to express his thanks to Dr. T. W. Olle of SHAPE Air Defence Technical Centre, The Hague, for his assistance in the translation and particularly to Mrs. J. M. Goldschmeding-Feringa of the Mathematical Centre, Amsterdam. Furthermore, thanks are due to Miss M. J. Bomers, also of the Mathematical Centre, for the accurate typing of the manuscript.

E. W. DIJKSTRA

JANUARY 1962

Contents

1. Introduction

ALGOL (derived from ALGOrithmic Language) is the name of a language which has been developed with the aim of describing computational processes. This language is defined so exactly, that an ALGOL description of a computational process is sufficient for a computer to perform its actual execution.

In the Computation Department of the Mathematical Centre in Amsterdam, a method has been developed for the computer there, the X1, to carry out computational processes described in ALGOL, known in short as ALGOL programs. The execution of an ALGOL program takes place in the following stages.

The text of the ALGOL program, written in accordance with the rules which we shall explain later, is typed out on a Flexowriter. This is an electric typewriter, on which everything that is typed is simultaneously punched out on seven-channel paper tape. The tape produced by the Flexowriter is a medium very similar to the somewhat narrower five-channel telex tape which is used in automatic telegraphy. Since the tape of the Flexowriter is broader, it can accommodate a larger number of different symbols than a telex tape. The Flexowriter distinguishes between capital and small letters, whereas the telex system recognizes only a single alphabet. In the following it will become apparent that we can make very good use of this larger number of symbols. Furthermore the Flexowriter can be used in order to type out automatically a text already punched out on a length of tape: besides a punching station the Flexowriter has also a reading station. A tape which is inserted in the reading station can be typed out and, if required, can also be punched out again. Hence the Flexowriter may also be used as a tape reproducer.

The tape that has been produced by the Flexowriter and now bears the text of the ALGOL program can be processed automatically by the X1. This processing takes place in two stages. The X1, for which a so-called 'compiler program' (the MC-translator) is available, can read the seven-hole tape containing the ALGOL text. While this text is being read, the ALGOL description is translated into a form that better meets the requirements imposed by the condition that the X1 shall carry out

1

the calculation efficiently. The result of this translation, which is always referred to as the 'object program', is punched out in the mean time. From an ALGOL program the translator derives an equivalent object program. Once this has taken place, the seven-hole tape containing the ALGOL text has done its work and, from then onwards, we use the tape which has been produced by the translator.

When the computation is to be carried out, we take the tape with the object program and insert this in the tape reader. This tape is read by a special input program, the information on the tape is recorded in the memory of the machine, and the machine is ready to carry out the required calculation.

The advantage of this arrangement is that the X1 has only to do the considerable amount of work involved in the translation once per problem. Other arrangements would have used more machine time and would have made heavier demands on the capacity of the memory. For the time being we shall not discuss the processing of the ALGOL tape any further. We shall first try to describe what the ALGOL language consists of and how one can use ALGOL in order to describe a process.

2. Assignment Statements

Let us start with a very simple example. At a certain moment it is required to calculate a quantity, f say, by forming the sum of two other quantities, say a and b. To a girl computor one would give, for example, the instruction:

'Calculate f = a + b.'

In ALGOL, which tries, where possible, to use customary notations, one would write:

$$f := a + b.$$

The symbol used here ':= ' (read 'becomes') has the function of a directed equality sign. It means that the left-hand member is defined in terms of the right, more precisely, that the variable on the left-hand side takes a value which is obtained by working out the right-hand side. For this reason a formula such as the one above is called an 'assignment statement'. (The term 'statement' is in ALGOL reserved for certain sections of the program, which, for some purposes, can be treated as separate units. As we proceed we shall come across the various kinds of statement. The assignment statement is thus named because it assigns a new value to a variable.)

If the assignment statement given above is to have any meaning it is necessary that, at the moment of its execution, the variables a and b should already have been given well-defined values (in previous assignment statements). This is not the case for the variable on the left side. If the variable f has not yet been used in the calculation, then its value will be undefined before the execution of this assignment statement; thereafter its value is equal to the sum of the values that a and b have at that moment. In principle, the variable f keeps this value until a later assignment statement assigns a new value to it. Thus the effect of the assignment statement is that any value that the left-hand variable may have had previously is lost: it is replaced by a new value.

The usual equality sign ' = ' is replaced by the 'becomes' sign ' := ' in order to emphasize the asymmetry. In the example given above, it is not so essential, because it is quite clear that the right-hand side is

3

the one which must be calculated, that it, therefore, does the defining, and, hence, that the left-hand side is the one which is to be defined. However, in the case of copying

$$f := a$$

it is desirable that some emphasis be placed on asymmetry.

The second reason is that, when you come to think about it, it is only fair to emphasize that we are dealing here with an operation which must be carried out and not, as with an equality sign, with a relation which is or is not satisfied. If, at a certain point of the calculation, we want to change the sign of an intermediate result, say e, then we do this with the assignment statement

$$e := -e;$$

If we had used an equality sign instead of a 'becomes' here, then we would have an equation with the single root e = 0, i.e., the very value for which a sign-change would be a pointless operation!

A special form of assignment statement is the so-called simultaneous assignment, in which the value of an expression is assigned to a number of variables, e.g.

$$`x := y := z := 1'$$

This means that x, y and z all take the value 1.

3. Identifiers and Numbers

In the examples given above we have indicated variables by letters, viz. a, b, e and f. These are the simplest examples of what are called identifiers. We shall see later that identifiers play a vital role, and that we use them not only to name variables, but, sometimes, groups of variables as well, points in the program, or even whole processes. It is therefore necessary that we should first describe what sort of structure identifiers in ALGOL may have.

In order to build up an identifier we have a choice of 62 symbols, to wit the 26 small letters a to z, the 26 capital letters A to Z and, finally, the ten digits 0 to 9. An identifier consists of an arbitrary number (at least one) of these symbols, but the first symbol may not be a digit. Permissible identifiers are, for example:

> q
> *eps*
> *Y3*
> *High pressure*
> *TENSION*
> *RK1ST*

The following sequences of symbols may not be used as identifiers:

> *K-point*
> *5th time*
> *note's*
> *art. 15.828*

The requirement that an identifier may not start with a digit makes it impossible to build up an identifier from digits only. This is very fortunate, because, otherwise, it would be impossible to decide whether the assignment statement

$$Rs := phi - 15$$

means that we must subtract from phi the number *15* or the variable which is identified by the name '*15*', in order to obtain the new value

5

of *Rs*. Since identifiers containing digits only are not permitted, it is quite clear that in this case the number fifteen is intended.

Another very reasonable convention is that spaces (and, what is more, carrying over to a new line) do not convey any information. The above identifier '*High pressure*' may thus also be written as '*Highpressure*' or even '*Hig hpr essure*'. In ALGOL this is a sequence of the same characters, and, for this reason, it is the same identifier.

In this connection we should like to stress that the capital letter *O* and the digit *0* are different symbols, despite the fact that they may be similar in handwriting and on a great number of typewriters. When one cannot differentiate sufficiently between these two, it is recommended that one should avoid the use of the capital letter *O* in all identifiers which may be chosen at one's own discretion. The same applies to the capital *I*, the small letter *l* and the digit *1*.

The language ALGOL does not itself place any limits on the maximum number of characters that may be used in an identifier. For practical reasons most translators have specific requirements on this point. For the MC-translator it is necessary that the first 9 symbols of an identifier are characteristic. An identifier may be longer, but, after the ninth symbol, the remaining symbols are ignored. Identifiers that differ only after the ninth symbol are hence treated by the MC-translator as being identical, with all the consequences thereof. (It is unwise to develop the habit of using such long identifiers. In the first place, the writing out of the ALGOL program becomes unnecessarily tedious. In the second place, the chance that the program would not be correctly treated by a translator for another machine increases, since the limit of the ninth symbol is much lower for most translators.)

Expressions may be formed from numbers as well as (the names of) variables, as we have seen in the last example. The numbers are written in the scale of ten, but the exact form is again governed by certain rules.

An unsigned number consists of a numerical part, possibly followed by a power of ten. The numerical part is either a whole number, consisting of at least one decimal digit, or a number with a fractional part, consisting of a number of decimal digits (at least one), one of which is preceded by a decimal point '.'. If required, the numerical parts may be followed by a whole power of ten; this consists of an integer exponent preceded by the special symbol '$_{10}$' (read as 'times ten to the power'). Another rule is that, in the case of an explicit decimal exponent, a numerical part equal to unity may be omitted. Examples of numbers are:

0	200.084	$3.1415\ 2653\ 7$
177	$+\ 07.43_{10}8$	$36\ 61\ 53$
$.5384$	$9.34_{10}+10$	$_{10}-4$
-0.7300	$2_{10}-4$	$-_{10}5$

N.B. Despite the normal pronunciation 'times ten to the power' one should not be led to regard the symbol '$_{10}$' as an operation sign. It is only part of the number notation like the decimal point, and supposed expressions such as

$$\text{`}ALPHA_{10}5\text{'}, \text{ `}-7_{10}\ delta\text{' or `}a_{10}b\text{'}$$

are not permitted.

4. Expressions

On the right-hand side of our assignment statements we can build up all sorts of expressions from variables and numbers. We have available the four normal algebraic operations: addition, subtraction, multiplication and division. They are indicated by the symbols '+', '−', '×' (or some other way of indicating the multiplication sign which is clearly distinguishable from the letter x, such as the asterisk which I recommend for manuscript) and '/'.

The use of these operation signs is governed by certain rules, the most important of which is that one may never omit the multiplication sign. The reason for this is quite clear. If we were allowed to write the assignment statement.

$$x := a \times b$$

as $x := ab$, then an ambiguity would be introduced into the ALGOL language: is the new value of x defined as the product of a and b, or as the value of the variable with the name 'ab', which might also occur in the calculation?

A consequence of the requirement that writing down the operation signs is obligatory is that the symbols composing the identifier or the number are always enclosed between two symbols which cannot belong either to the identifier or to the number. This makes it possible for the translator to detect where the identifier begins and where it ends. For the same reason, the multiplication sign may not be replaced by a decimal point, for we could not then be able to differentiate between the number 15·5 ($= 31/2$) and the product 15×5 ($= 75$).

Hence when we assert that, in ALGOL, arithmetic expressions may be written according to the normal algebraic notation, then we mean 'apart from the usual ambiguities, which are permitted in the case of a human reader, but not in the case of a machine'. Any physicist or chemist will recognize the relationship 'PV=RT' as the law of Boyle and Gay-Lussac. But one cannot expect a machine to divine from these symbols that this concerns an equality of two products.

N.B. It follows from the above that use of the multiplication sign is also obligatory even if the first factor is a number. The nth odd natural

8

number is given in ALGOL by '$2 \times n - 1$' and not by the much more usual '2n-1'.

A less fundamental convention concerns the relative priority of the operations. Multiplication and division have priority over addition and subtraction; otherwise the operations are carried out from left to right.

Examples:

$eps := C + BIR \times BAR$ means $eps := C + (BIR \times BAR)$
$Sg := x / l - x$ means $Sg := (x / l) - x$
$prod := a / b \times c$ means $prod := (a / b) \times c$

Multiplication thus has no priority over division.

The rules of priority, such as those above, are only a means of reducing the number of brackets, but sometimes we cannot avoid using these. (Brackets which, thanks to the rules of priority, are unnecessary, may be omitted, but do not have to be.)

The normal form for the following assignment statement is

$$y := (1 + x) / (1 - x)$$

but, if the programmer prefers to do so, he may also write

$$y := (((1) + x)) / ((1 - ((x)))) .$$

When brackets are enclosed within brackets, one keeps on using ordinary round brackets and does not resort to square or larger brackets.

Algebraic brackets are normally mentioned in connection with priority. One learns to use the rule of thumb 'first work out the innermost brackets'. In the product in

$$x := (a + b) \times (c + d)$$

the sums $a + b$ and $c + d$ must first be formed before the multiplication can take place.

With a view to later applications, it appears worthwhile to elucidate the effect of brackets in a slightly different way. Of course the rule 'work out innermost brackets first' leads naturally enough to the correct answer, but, in fact, it merely gives the (arithmetic) consequence of the meaning of the brackets and not their meaning itself. The fundamental function of algebraic brackets is that whatever they enclose, however complicated it may be, is shielded from the outside world, so that, from outside, it can be regarded as an ordinary variable with nothing special about it.

When we say that in the assignment statement given above the quantity x must be calculated as the product of two sums, this is indeed correct, but a little bit too detailed: in the first instance we would only observe that x is given as a product, and how we get the factors is (by virtue of the brackets) another matter. It is as if we had had

$$x := v1 \times v2$$

We come across this aspect straight away in considering the arithmetic operation of raising numbers to a power. It has been customary so far to write the exponent somewhat higher than the base. We have seen that a space and a new line do not convey any information in ALGOL and, in the same way, it is not an attractive proposition to have to derive vital information from the fact that symbols 'wobble up and down the line'. In order to avoid all misunderstanding a new operator '↑' (read as 'to the power') is introduced. Hence '$a \uparrow b$' means 'a to the power b'.

Raising a number to the power has a higher priority than multiplication and division. Note that ordinary variables and unsigned numbers may appear both in the base and in the exponent, but that brackets must be used as soon as these are more complicated expressions, in order to indicate clearly where the base begins and where the exponent ends. Hence, one would write

$$c := a \uparrow 2 + b \uparrow 2 \text{ instead of } c := a^2 + b^2,$$

but

$$a^{2r} + 1$$

becomes, in ALGOL 60,

$$a \uparrow (2 \times r) + 1,$$

whereas

$$x^{-2} \text{ becomes } x \uparrow (-2).$$

Had we omitted the brackets in last two examples, then the first one would be interpreted as

$$(a \uparrow 2) \times r + 1, \text{ meaning } (a^2) \times r + 1,$$

and the latter one would have given rise to an incorrect ALGOL formula.

The moral of this is, of course, that one should not hesitate to insert brackets at all points where one is not absolutely sure how the priority rules will interpret the expression without them. By doing so one reduces the chance of making mistakes, increases the readability of one's ALGOL program for those who are not so familiar with the finer points of the language, and, finally, it can never do any harm. The MC-translator has the property that any pair of brackets that is, linguistically speaking, redundant, does not have the slightest influence on the object program. It cannot be seen from the object program whether the translator has taken its decisions on account of the brackets, or on account of the priority rules.

5. Sequence of Statements

So far we have confined ourselves to small examples consisting of single assignment statements. Very soon, however, one needs more than one assignment statement in order to formulate even a part of a calculation. Suppose that we want to multiply the complex number z = x + yi by 0.6 + 0.8i, and that this product is again to be called z. In ALGOL, however, it is not possible to represent a complex number by an identifier. This implies that we must formulate this complex multiplication in terms of the real and imaginary parts. A slight complication is that, if we first calculate the new real part, we still need the old real part in order to form the new imaginary part. If, on the other hand, we first define the new imaginary part we are confronted by a similar difficulty. The solution is obtained by the introduction of an auxiliary variable. We can program the multiplication by the following three ALGOL statements.

$$u := 0.6 \times x - 0.8 \times y;$$
$$y := 0.8 \times x + 0.6 \times y;$$
$$x := u$$

The arithmetic described here speaks for itself. The only new feature is the use of the semicolon ';' between successive statements. The semicolon is called in ALGOL the 'statement separator': all successive statements must be separated from each other by the symbol ';'.

It is clear that in general such a separating symbol is essential. One statement can end with an identifier, and the next statement can begin with an identifier. If these statements were to follow upon each other without any separating symbol, the translator would not be able to detect where the last identifier in the first statement ends and where the first indentifier in the following statement begins. Our assertion above 'that each identifier is always enclosed between two symbols that cannot be part of an identifier' implies such a convention. With the introduction of the semicolon this is achieved on a higher level, i.e. for the statements: each statement is enclosed between two symbols which cannot be a part of the statement itself.

6. Statement Brackets

In the same way as identifiers in a statement are separated from each other by operators, the successive statements in a piece of ALGOL text are separated by the separator ';' (or, if you like, by the operator ';', having the meaning 'and proceed to the next statement'). But the analogy goes further. We have seen that, in an expression, a number of identifiers, separated from each other by operators, can be grouped together inside a pair of algebraic brackets, which make the enclosed sub-expression a (syntactical) unit with respect to its environment. In exactly the same way two brackets have been introduced, i.e. the symbol 'begin' as statement opening bracket and the symbol 'end' as statement closing bracket.

Before considering the function of the statement brackets **begin** and **end** further, we must explain the role played by the words in bold type. We have already met about 70 so-called basic symbols of ALGOL, i.e. the 26 small letters, the 26 capital letters, 10 digits, the operators := + − × / and ↑, the brackets (and) and the separators ; $_{10}$ and . . ALGOL requires a considerably larger number of basic symbols, and in order to overcome, once and for all, the typographical difficulties which might arise, a mechanism was introduced for the creation of new symbols. This mechanism consists of a specific interpretation of bold type. By writing '**begin**' we denote a specific ALGOL symbol which has nothing to do with the five letters, b, e, g, i and n. The convention of bold type promotes this configuration to a new basic symbol. In this way about 20 new symbols are introduced. (The use of bold type is only one way in which we can represent these additional symbols: in a written or typed ALGOL program − where bold type letters are not available − it is customary to represent these symbols by underlining the letter combinations. The Flexowriters, on which we produce our ALGOL program tapes, are fitted with an underlining facility by means of a non-escaping key.)

The first use of the statement brackets **begin** and **end** is to show where the ALGOL program begins and where the text ends. By convention we start the ALGOL program with the symbol **begin** and finish it with the symbol **end**. (The official ALGOL rules appear to permit the omission of these all-embracing statement brackets in some exceptional cases. The MC-translator always requires them.) The statement brackets are used exclusively in neatly 'nested' pairs, i.e. each opening bracket must be followed later by a corresponding closing bracket, and which opening and closing brackets belong to each other can be concluded from the fact that the bracket pairs must contain each other. When the translator reads the text from beginning to end, it can ascertain for each closing bracket to which opening bracket it corresponds. Hence, when the translator finds the closing bracket **end** which is the partner of the very first **begin**, then it knows at the same time that the whole ALGOL program has been read.

Let us now make a few necessary additions to our example of the complex multiplication. Apart from adding the all-embracing statement brackets, we have to give the real and imaginary part some value before the multiplication can be carried out, because otherwise the expressions would not be defined. Our example has, for instance, grown into:

> **begin**
> $$x := 5 \ / \ 13; y := 12 \ / \ 13;$$
> $$u := 0.6 \times x - 0.8 \times y;$$
> $$y := 0.8 \times x + 0.6 \times y;$$
> $$x := u$$
> **end**

7. Type Declarations

There is no harm in the fact that the example given at the end of the last chapter does not deliver any result to the outside world, but allows me to stress that the text does not yet satisfy all the requirements. The calculation in question is only described correctly in ALGOL if we write:

$$\begin{aligned}
&\textbf{begin}\quad \textbf{real } x, y, u; \\
&\qquad x := 5/13; y := 12/13; \\
&\qquad u := 0.6 \times x - 0.8 \times y; \\
&\qquad y := 0.8 \times x + 0.6 \times y; \\
&\qquad x := u \\
&\textbf{end}
\end{aligned}$$

The line that was inserted before the first assignment statement is not a statement, but what is called a declaration. (Until now we have referred to the symbol ';' as a statement separator. This was too restricted, because the semicolon separates both statements and declarations). The function of the declaration given above is nothing more than an announcement that the identifiers x, y and u may be used in the subsequent text to refer to normal, real variables. The obligation of announcing this so explicitly in front of the statements may seem somewhat unnecessary at present, as up till now such variables have been the only objects referred to by identifiers. In ALGOL, however, other objects of other types occur, to which we also wish to refer by means of an identifier. When these also appear in a program, it is very convenient to know beforehand in which sense the identifiers are going to be used.

The requirement that a declaration should announce in advance the type of meaning the identifier is going to have is not so surprising if one realizes that ALGOL is a language for which only the structure is specified, but for which the vocabulary may be chosen, to a very large extent, by the user. In everyday life we usually do not come across this problem, because in our languages most words have a fairly fixed meaning. But, for example, the fact that 'Pietje' is a girl's name in a small part of the Netherlands, but definitely a boy's name in the remaining parts of the country, has, as one can imagine, caused the expected amount of confusion. Perhaps it is illuminating to realize that such a situation occurs in ALGOL for nearly every identifier.

The **real** declaration consists of the symbol 'real' followed by one or more identifiers. If more than one identifier is listed, these are separated by a comma ','. After the last identifier on the list, there is a semicolon, which separates the declaration as a whole from the following declaration or statement. Here we have met the comma for the first time; it is used in ALGOL to separate the individual elements in a list, in this case a list of identifiers.

Analogous to the **real** declaration, ALGOL admits the **integer** declaration. This consists of the symbol 'integer', followed by one or more identifiers. In the case of more identifiers, the elements are again separated by a comma. Apart from the fact that the one declaration starts with the symbol **real** and the other with the symbol **integer**, the structure of both declarations is the same.

The **integer** declaration implies that the identifiers concerned refer to variables that may take on integer values only. On integer declared variables the MC-translator imposes the restriction that their absolute value must be less than $67108864 = 2 \uparrow 26$. A compensation for this restriction is that we know for certain that the values of these variables will be represented exactly during the execution of the ALGOL program. Exact representation is explicitly not guaranteed for **real** declared variables. In using ALGOL, we must bear in mind that all **real** declared variables are represented to a finite precision only and that, in consequence, we may not expect any arithmetic operation on these variables to be carried out exactly. Although the official ALGOL refrains from any further details on purpose, we may regard the value of a **real** declared variable as being represented to a fixed relative precision. What this relative precision is, is a characteristic of the system (machine, translator, etc.) that carries out the ALGOL program. A good ALGOL program makes as few suppositions as possible about these specific properties of an actual system.

In most cases the fact that the exact form of number representation and of the arithmetic is uncertain, does not cause the slightest difficulty. Where difficulties do occur, they can usually be put down to the basic problems of numerical mathematics, and one cannot blame ALGOL for the fact that such cases occur. Sometimes these problems can be solved by the introduction of variables declared by an **integer** declaration. Here one purchases exact representation at the price of a limited range of values. For the specific application of integers (counters and subscripts) this limitation is hardly a restriction.

With regard to arithmetical operations, ALGOL specifies that the result of the division 'a/b' is always of the type **real**, even if both a and b are of type **integer** and the division happens to be exact. The results of the addition '$a + b$', of the subtraction '$a - b$' and of the multiplication '$a \times b$' is of type **integer** only if both a and b are of this type. Again the MC-translator imposes the condition that the absolute value of the result must be less than the upper limit 67108864 (as above); if this extra condition is not fulfilled, then a transfer to **real** representation automatically takes place.

Let us now examine the assignment statement:

$$\text{`} x := \text{E'}$$

in which E is some sort of expression. If the arithmetic evaluation of the expression E gives a result of the type **integer**, when x has already been declared an **integer**, then the function of this assignment statement is quite unambiguous.

If the evaluation of the expression E gives a result of type **real** and x is a **real** declared variable, then we have to give a more detailed description of what is happening. It is true that the admitted range of the absolute value of a **real** declared variable is very large, but, after all, nobody has ever said that this range runs from zero to infinity. The following is valid for the MC-translator:
The modulus of a **real** declared variable has a fixed lower bound of about $10 \uparrow (- 600)$ and a fixed upper bound of about $10 \uparrow (+ 600)$. The modulus of the real result E, however, has—as all intermediate results of type real—a lower lower bound, viz. about $10 \uparrow (-_{10}7)$ and a higher upper bound, viz. about $10 \uparrow (+_{10}7)$. If, at the moment of assignment, the absolute value of E happens to lie outside the more restricted range of the **real** declared variables, the value of E is replaced by the nearest of these bounds. Furthermore, it is quite possible that the result E so formed has a larger number of digits than is available to represent the variable x: in this case our assignment includes round-off.

If the evaluation of the expression E gives a result of type **integer**, but x is a **real** declared variable, then ALGOL 60 requires that such an assignment should include a transfer to the **real** representation. Although **real** declared variables can only be represented to a finite precision, it must be added that, in the MC-translator, the **real** declared variable

x will represent the integer value of E exactly, at least as long as the value of E is not equal to zero.

Conversely, if the evaluation of E gives a result of type **real**, while the variable x is of type **integer**, then assigning a value to this quantity implies rounding-off to the nearest whole number. If this value lies outside the permitted range, then the program stops. One should note that, in consequence of the finite precision of results of type **real**, the effect of the assignment statement

$$`x := 7/2`$$

for an **integer** declared variable x is undefined: x could just as well be $= 3$ as $= 4$. In a simultaneous assignment, all variables to the left of the 'becomes' sign must be of the same type.

In order to facilitate integer arithmetic, a special integer division has been introduced, indicated by the sign '$\underline{:}$'. (The official representation of this division sign consists of the superposition of ':' and '$-$'. For technical reasons we shall indicate this by underlining the colon.) The quotient '$m\underline{:}n$' is only defined if the m and n are both of type **integer**. For $n = 0$ the quotient '$m\underline{:}n$' is undefined. In all other cases the result is of type **integer** and the numerical value is equal to the quotient corresponding to the remainder of minimum absolute value and, if the remainder is not equal to zero, of the same sign as m. The remainder itself is lost. (The following holds for absolute values:

$$|m/n| - 1 < |m\underline{:}n| \leqq |m/n|;$$

It should be noted that in this definition the expression m/n represents the exact value of the mathematical quotient and not this value expressed with only a finite accuracy.)

We are now going to extend our earlier example. The attentive reader will not have failed to observe that the complex number $z = x + yi$, which originally had a modulus equal to unity, was multiplied by a factor $0.6 + 0.8i$, which also has a modulus equal to unity. Hence the new z must also have a modulus of one and must retain this if z is repeatedly multiplied by this factor. That is to say, mathematically, the modulus remains exactly equal to 1, numerically, however, the modulus only remains approximately equal to 1. The divergence is caused by round-off during the calculation and possibly also because the real and imaginary parts of $0.6 + 0.8i$ may not be represented exactly. (One should realize that the fractions 0.6 and 0.8 are recurrent fractions in the binary scale.)

If we carry out the multiplication by $0.6 + 0.8i$ repeatedly, we get an idea of the 'quality' of the arithmetic by examining the rate at which the modulus of z deviates from unity.

8. 'go to' Statements

One way of carrying out the multiplication of z repeatedly is writing out the three assignment statements which describe the complex multiplication several times. If this multiplication is to be carried out a large number of times, this technique would make writing an ALGOL program more like writing punishment lines at school than work that pretends to be intelligent. What we wish to express in the language is something like 'and now exactly as above'. We can express this idea with the help of a special sort of statement, called a '**go to** statement'. (Here use is made of a new symbol **go to**; this, again, is introduced by bold type. If this symbol is represented using underlining, the space in between should be underlined as well. At the Mathematical Centre, it has gradually become a habit to omit the space and to write the symbol as '**goto**'. By doing so, we once again emphasize the fact that we are here dealing with a single symbol.) While statements, as a rule, are obeyed in the order in which they occur in the text, the **goto** statement gives us the opportunity of breaking this sequence, by indicating some other (for the present) arbitrary statement as the next one to be obeyed.

The statement which, by the execution of a **goto** statement, becomes the next to be obeyed, must for this purpose be provided with what is called a label. Any identifier may be chosen as label, with the natural restriction that it may not be an identifier with some other meaning. One labels a statement by writing a label before the statement and separating it from this statement by a colon ':'. Continuation of the process, by a jump to this labelled statement, is effected by a **goto** statement, which must consist of the symbol '**goto**' followed by the label in question.

N.B. Labels do not need to be declared in advance. Their occurrence in the text, followed by a symbol ':' at the point where a statement may begin, is a sufficient indication that this identifier will be used as a label in this context. (According to the official ALGOL report, whole numbers without a sign may be used as labels as well, but the MC-translator requires that, for labels, normal identifiers, beginning with a letter, must be chosen.)

The program that repeatedly multiplies z by 0.6 + 0.8i now takes the following form:

```
begin  real x, y, u;
        x := 5/13; y := 12/13;
AA:     u := 0.6 × x − 0.8 × y;
        y := 0.8 × x + 0.6 × y;
        x := u; goto AA
end
```

9. Conditional Statements

We were completely free in the choice of the label identifier AA. We notice that the program now contains one extra statement and that, as a result, the text contains one more semicolon. Now the above program would go on multiplying indefinitely, and it is quite likely that, in fact, what is required is to carry out the multiplication a preset number of times, say 1000, in order to see how far the modulus of z has deviated from 1 in the meantime. This means that the **goto** statement, which effects the repetition, would have to be performed the first 999 times, but that then the process should stop, i.e. that then the **goto** statement should be skipped. In other words, this statement must not be carried out unconditionally, since there may be circumstances in which it should have no effect. ALGOL consequently provides the possibility of transforming a statement into what is called a 'conditional statement'. The condition, which must be satisfied if the statement is to be carried out, is placed immediately before the statement; such a condition is introduced by the symbol '**if**' and terminated by the symbol '**then**'. If the condition inserted between these two is not fulfilled, then the statement that follows the symbol '**then**' is skipped.

The program that carries out the multiplication 1000 times now takes on the following form:

```
begin   real x, y, u; integer k;
        x := 5/13;  y:= 12/13;  k:= 0;
AA:     u := 0.6 × x − 0.8 × y;
        y := 0.8 × x + 0.6 × y;
        x := u;
        k := k + 1;  if k < 1000 then goto AA
end
```

In this example, the so-called 'if clause' (i.e. the text from **if** up to and including **then**) is followed by a **goto** statement, but it might just as well have been followed by an assignment statement. If, in the course of a calculation, it is required to replace the quantity called

22

'*Tol*' by its absolute value, then one may write the conditional statement as

        '**if** $Tol < 0$ **then** $Tol := -Tol$'.

The **if** clause functions as prefix to the assignment statement and hence does not require an extra semicolon.

Very often the operation to be carried out conditionally cannot be formulated in a single statement as above. For example, it may be required to change the sign of the variables '*Tel*' and '*Tal*', if '*Tol*' is negative. It is in such circumstances that the use of the statement brackets **begin** and **end** is seen to full advantage: the statements, which together describe the conditional operation, are introduced by the opening bracket **begin** and closed by a closing bracket **end**. By thus 'shielding' the compound we ensure that, from the outside, it is regarded as a single statement, in this case the statement which has the **if** clause as prefix. The operation of changing the sign of '*Tel*' and '*Tal*' with the above condition is formulated in ALGOL as follows:

        '**if** $Tol < 0$ **then begin** $Tel := -Tel$; $Tal := -Tal$ **end**'.

The piece from **begin** up to and including **end** has taken the place of a single statement. Note that the only semicolon in the above text is the one separating the two inner statements of the compound statement.

There is one more case in which the use of an **if** clause gives rise to an extra pair of statement brackets. The statement following the **if** clause may not itself be conditional. (The reason for this will become clear later). Hence, if we wish to replace '*Tel*' by its absolute value if '*Tol*' is negative, then we could write:

        '**if** $Tol < 0$ **then begin if** $Tel < 0$ **then** $Tel := -Tel$ **end**'.

The condition in the **if** clause is formulated here as a relation between two quantities, and the relation may or may not be satisfied. ALGOL 60 recognizes 6 different relations, i.e.:

        '$<$' less than
        '$\leq$' less than or equal to
        '$=$' equal to
        '$\geq$' greater than or equal to
        '$>$' greater than
        '$\neq$' not equal to.

So far these relational operators have only been used between simple variables and numbers, but they may also be used between arbitrarily chosen arithmetic expressions, e.g.

'**if** $a + b = c + d$ **then**'
'**if** $Flip \times Flop \leq Flap \uparrow 2$ **then**' etc.

The exact meaning of these conditions is quite clear if the expressions that occur on both sides of the relation sign are of type **integer**. If one of them is of type **integer** and the other is of type **real**, a transfer function from **integer** to **real** representation is called into action by the MC-translator, and as a result two real results are compared.

The MC-translator only regards two real results as being equal if they are completely identical. In other words, finite accuracy for real variables is not so much taken into account in their representation, in their 'individuality', as it is in the arithmetic operations in which they are formed. Note that the condition '$a - b = 0$' may be satisfied for non-identical values of a and b, i.e. values such that '$a = b$' is not satisfied.

So far we have used the **if** clause to carry out a statement, or not. The **if** clause, however, can be used in another way, viz. to decide which of two alternative statements should be executed. In this case the **if** clause is followed by that statement which will only be carried out if the condition is fulfilled, but by means of the symbol '**else**' this statement is now connected to a next statement which will only be carried out if the condition is not satisfied. Indicating the conditions by B1, B2, etc. and the statements by S1, S2, etc., we have

'**if** B1 **then** S1 ; S2'

which results in S1 being carried out only if the condition E1 is satisfied, but S2 always being executed, whereas

'**if** B1 **then** S1 **else** S2; S3'

signifies that S1 will only be executed if the condition B1 is satisfied, S2 if the condition B1 is not satisfied and that S3 will always be executed. Hence, one can regard the effect of **else** as omitting the execution of S2 in the case that S1 is indeed obeyed. It follows from this that if S1 is a **goto** statement, the symbol **else** can be replaced by a semicolon without affecting the meaning of the program. (The effect of the ALGOL program is not influenced by this, and in the case of a semicolon the MC-translator compiles a somewhat shorter program.)

In contrast to S1, S2 may take on one of the two forms of the conditional statement. The statements

'if B1 **then** S1 **else if** B2 **then** S3; S5'

and

'if B1 **then** S1 **else if** B2 **then** S3 **else** S4; S5'

can only be interpreted in one way. If B1 is satisfied, then in both cases S1 and thereafter S5 are executed. If B1 is not satisfied but B2 is, then in both cases S3 and S5 are executed. If neither condition is satisfied, then the first example results in S5 only and the second example results in S4 followed by S5.

It is now quite clear why the statement S1, i.e. the statement following the symbol **then,** may not be conditional itself. If this were allowed, the following construction would be permitted:

'if B1 **then if** B2 **then** S6 **else** S7; S8',

which could be explained in two ways, i.e.

'if B1 **then begin if** B2 **then** S6 **else** S7 **end**; S8'

and

'if B1 **then begin if** B2 **then** S6 **end else** S7; S8'.

For purposes of clarification we now give a piece of program in which a variable called MAX is assigned the value of the largest of three variables, which are identified by a, b and c.

> **'if** $a < b$ **then**
> **begin if** $b < c$ **then** $MAX := c$ **else** $MAX := b$ **end**
> **else**
> **if** $a < c$ **then** $MAX := c$ **else** $MAX := a$'

Regarded from the outside, the program has taken the form of a single conditional statement of the second type. In passing, attention must be drawn to the fact that, in spite of the occurrence of four assignment statements, the statement separator ';' does not appear.

10. for Statements

We now give yet a further form of the ALGOL program, in which the complex number x + yi is multiplied a thousand times by 0.6 + 0.8i. In it we introduce four new ALGOL symbols, i.e. 'for', 'do', 'step' and 'until'. The new version of our example is as follows:

begin   real $x, y, u;$ **integer** $k;$
$x := 5/13; y := 12/13;$
for $k := 1$ **step** 1 **until** 1000 **do**
begin $u := 0.6 \times x - 0.8 \times y;$
$y := 0.8 \times x + 0.6 \times y;$
$x := u$
    end
end

The portion 'for $k := 1$ **step** 1 **until** 1000 **do**' is a so-called 'for clause'. A **for** clause signifies that a series of values is given in succession to a variable (in this case, to the integer k, which is initially given the value 1, and, thereafter, all values at increments of 1 up to, and including 1000) and that for each of these values of k, the statement which follows the symbol '**do**' must be executed once. A **for** clause followed by a statement are together referred to as a **for** statement. The introduction of the **for** statement is not a fundamental enrichment of ALGOL, because everything which can be expressed by a **for** statement, can also be expressed with the help of other statements without making use of a **for** clause. However, the need to repeat a statement a number of times is encountered so frequently, that we must regard the **for** statement as an exceptionally useful abbreviation. Once one has become accustomed to the **for** statement, one will notice that its use tends considerably to increase the degree of readability of programs.

The action to be repeated is given by the statement that follows the symbol **do**. If the action is described by a number of statements, as in our case it is by three assignment statements, then these statements are enclosed in statement brackets **begin** and **end**, in exactly the same way as was done in the case of the conditional statement. The analogy with the **if** clause goes further, because the statement following the **for** clause may also not be a conditional statement. (This restriction is also made in order to force the programmer to use the statement brackets in such a case, thereby avoiding any possible ambiguity.)

The example given above makes only partial use of the possibilities of **for** statements. Here the **for** statement has the function of a counter (repeat the following statement 1000 times) and no use is made of the fact that, during the first execution of the repeated statement, $k = 1$, during the second execution, $k = 2$, etc. Use of this fact is illustrated in the following program which approximates e (the base of natural logarithms) by the summation of consecutive inverse factorials, in this case up to and including the 20th.

```
begin   real eprox, term; integer n;
        eprox := term := 1;
        for n := 1 step 1 until 20 do
        begin   term :=  term / n;
                eprox := eprox + term;
        end
end
```

The range of values of the controlled variable (in this case the **integer** n, but it may also be a **real** declared variable) is given by what is called a '**step-until** element' here, the structure of which is given by

'initial value **step** increment **until** final limit'.

I have on purpose avoided using the term 'end value', because the variable does not necessarily take on this last value: the **step-until** element is regarded as finished as soon as the final limit has been passed. Hence the element

'0 **step** 3 **until** 24'

is equivalent to the element

'0 **step** 3 **until** 25.73'

because in both cases 24 is the last value, since the next value (27) has passed the final limit.

We have not called the final limit 'the upper limit', because the increment may be negative, e.g.

'10 **step** − 2 **until** 4'

gives the controlled variable the values 10, 8, 6, 4 in this order.

The quantities which we indicate here by 'initial value', 'increment' and 'final limit' were numbers in the previous example. Arbitrary expressions, however, are allowed instead of numbers. In these expressions, variables may occur the value of which may be changed in the repeated statement. To complicate the matter still further, the increment and the final boundary may be functions of the controlled variable. This is not the place to describe in full detail the implications of the **step-until** element in these circumstances. These are laid down exactly in the official ALGOL report, more for the benefit of those who are going to construct a translator, than for the users of ALGOL, who generally do not require such sophisticated constructions. Nevertheless, we shall elaborate this matter a little further.

We consider the **for** statement, symbolically represented by

'**for** CV := A **step** B **until** C **do** S1'

where CV represents the controlled variable and S1 the statement to be repeated. The initial value, increment and final boundary are given by A, B and C respectively. In general these may be expressions. The specific **step-until** mechanism comes into action before every next (possible) execution of the statement S1. In the **step-until** mechanism we must distinguish between two different values of CV, the old one and the new one. The first time the mechanism comes into use only the new value is defined explicitly and CV is made equal to the initial value A; thereafter the new value of CV is computed by means of

'CV := CV + B'

If the increment B is an expression dependent on the value of CV, this is necessarily the old value of CV, as the new one has not yet been formed. If the final limit C depends on CV, then this is dependent on the new value of CV. Before the statement S1 is to be executed (or not) with the new value of CV, an investigation is made to see whether the **step-until** element is exhausted due to the passing of the final limit. The element is considered to be completely finished as soon as the inequality

$$0 < B \times (CV - C)$$

is satisfied. In order to carry out this test, we need the value (principally the sign) of the increment B. The case CV = A is also subjected to this test, i.e. when we begin the **step-until** element (and do not need the value of the increment B for the formation of the new CV). In the following case 'for $k := 0$ step 1 until n do S; S2'

where k and n are **integer** declared variables, S1 is executed n + 1 times for non-negative values of n and not at all for negative values of n. In other words, the 'empty cycle' is catered for.

The reader should now work out how often and with which successive values of k the statement S1 is executed in the following example:

> **begin integer** k, m, n;
> . . . . . . ;
> $n := expression$;
> $m := 11$;
> **for** $k := 0$ **step** m **until** n **do begin** S1; $m := m - 1$ **end**
> **end**

when no assignments to n, m and k occur outside the given places; and this should be investigated for the following values of 'expression': $-$ 10, 0, 5, 30, 53, 54, 55 and 56.

The above example contains one **step-until** element between the 'becomes' sign and the symbol **do.** There may, however, be more here. They are then separated by a comma and executed from left to right. Hence

> 'for $LIM := 0$ step 2 until 100 do S1; S2'

is equivalent to

> 'for $LIM := 0$ **step** 2 **until** $30, 32$ **step** 2 **until** 100 do S1; S2'.

A more sensible application would be in the construction of a table with different intervals, something like:

> 'for $arg := 0$ **step** $.01$ **until** $.5, .52$ **step** $.02$ **until** 1 **do** . . . .'.

In the place of the **step-until** element we may have simpler things, i.e. a single value or what is known as a **while** element.

The single value is, in general, an expression. Its value is assigned to the controlled variable, the statement following the **do** is executed once, and then the program checks whether further values for the controlled variable are defined in the **for** clause.

Assuming that the statement S does not change the value of the controlled variable, we may write

> 'for $k := - 5$ **step** 3 **until** $+ 7$ **do** S1; S2'

as

> 'for $k := - 5, - 2, 1, + 4, 7$ **do** S1; S2'

or, less elegantly, as

> 'for $k := - 5, k + 3, + 1$ **step** $+ 3$ **until** 7 **do** S1; S2'.

The **while** element consists of an arithmetic expression followed by the new symbol 'while', which in its turn is followed by a condition. The **while** element implies that the arithmetic expression is evaluated, the value obtained is assigned to the controlled variable, the statement following the **do** is executed, after which the expression is worked out again, and the value obtained assigned to the controlled variable, etc. The fact that this process would continue in this manner ad infinitum explains why the condition introduced by the **while** is added. Just before the statement following the **do** is to be executed, a test is made to see whether the condition in question is satisfied. If so, the procedure is as described above. If not, then the process ends and the **while** element is regarded as exhausted. With the help of the **while** element we can now formulate our last example as follows:

$$\text{'for } k := -5, k + 3 \text{ while } k \leq 7 \text{ do S1}; \text{S2'}.$$

In general the becomes sign in the **for** clause is followed by a list of 'elements', each separated by a comma, and terminated by the symbol **do**. We have seen three types, the **step-until** element, the single value and the **while** element, and these three types may alternate with each other in any way. When the last element of the list has been dealt with, the whole **for** statement is regarded as completely executed.

The statement following the **do** can be labelled, or, if this statement consists of a number of other statements, each separated from the other by semicolons, the whole being contained between the statement brackets **begin** and **end**, then any of the 'inner statements' may be labelled. The statement following the symbol **do** (i.e. the piece which is to be repeated) is called 'the range of the **for** statement'. It is forbidden to enter the range of a **for** statement by means of a **goto** statement from outside the range of this **for** statement.

On the other hand, a **goto** statement can stand inside the range of a **for** statement, and may lead to a labelled statement outside. The **for** statement is then regarded as completed, and the value of the controlled variable is equal to the value it had just before the completion of the **goto** statement. This must be stated explicitly, because in the case where the **for** statement is completed due to exhaustion of the last element, the value of the controlled variable is undefined.

(The report states that the final value of the controlled variable after the exhaustion of a **step-until** element or a **while** element is undefined. This was done with the intention of giving implementors more freedom, e.g. the choice between the last value accepted or the first one rejected. As one might need the new value of the controlled variable in examining the condition, translators have no choice in this respect. I therefore regard the rule, that the value of the controlled variable is undefined after using the last element in the list, as a mistake. In the MC-translator, the value of the controlled variable after finishing one element in the **for** clause, is indeed firmly defined. For a single value it is this value, for the two other kinds of elements, it is the first value rejected, provided, of course, that no other assignment to the controlled variable has occurred in the mean time.)

The reader should realize that the list element in

$$\text{`for } x := a \text{ step } b \text{ until } x \text{ do} \ldots \ldots \text{'}$$

is never exhausted. Unless this **for** statement is terminated by leaving its range via a **goto** statement, this **for** statement never ends.

11. Special Functions

Nine identifiers in ALGOL 60 have a special meaning, i.e. the identifiers reserved for the following standard functions. The argument, which is placed between brackets after the name of the function, may be an arbitrary arithmetic expression. Such an expression is indicated below by 'E'.

abs (E) = the absolute value (the modulus) of the value of the expression E.

sign (E) = the 'sign' of the value of E (i.e. = + 1 if E is positive, = 0 if E is zero, and = − 1 if E is negative).

sqrt (E) = the square root of the value of E.

sin (E) = the sine of the value of E.

cos (E) = the cosine of the value of E.

arctan (E) = the principal value of the arctangent of the value of E.

ln (E) = the natural logarithm of the value of E.

exp (E) = the exponential function of the value of E.

entier (E) = the largest whole number not greater than the value of E.

The arguments of these nine functions may be either of type **integer** or of type **real**. For the function abs, the result is of the same type as the argument. For the functions sign and entier, the result is always of type **integer**. For the other six the result is always of type **real**. (This applies to the MC-translator; in official ALGOL 60, the result of the function 'abs' is always **real**, even if the argument is of type **integer**.)

If an argument (for sin and cos) or the result (for arctan) can be interpreted as an angle, then the angle is naturally measured in radians. Of course, the base of the logarithm and the exponential function is e.

The MC-translator differs from the official ALGOL report in another minor aspect. The functions sqrt and ln in the MC-translator operate on the absolute value of the given argument. We chose to do this in order to obviate difficulties which otherwise could occur when a mathematically very small positive number has become just less than zero on account of rounding-off.

N.B. *abs* (E) = E × *sign* (E) holds .

32

As has already been stated, ALGOL 60 is, in the first instance, a language which was developed in order to describe numerical processes. If one wishes to use this language for the documentation of computing techniques, then ALGOL 60 is complete as it stands and serves this purpose very well. It even serves it so well that we want to do more with it. We want to be able to describe a numerical process in ALGOL 60 and, given this description only, to let a computer perform this process. But that we are interested in the actual execution of a process will nearly always imply that we are also interested in the results. In the description of the process to be carried out we therefore wish to be able to indicate which results the computer must deliver to the outside world. On this matter, the official ALGOL 60 report is as silent as the grave, and with very good reason.

One cannot adequately fulfil this requirement simply by indicating which results must be output, for the ways in which this can be done will depend to a large extent on the specific nature of the communication equipment available. For example, the X1 is equipped with an on-line electrical typewriter and we shall use this typewriter to let the X1 produce the results in printed form. But everybody knows that the length of a typewriter carriage is finite, i.e. it is not sufficient merely to specify the numbers which must be printed out, we must also say when we wish to start on a new line. This problem would not arise if the machine were equipped with the printing mechanism of an accounting machine, which prints all the numbers under each other on a strip of paper. Since one must now not only indicate which results must be printed, but, also, how they must be printed, and, since the specifications differ so very much from one computing machine to another, the problem has deliberately been left outside the ALGOL 60 language. This has been done on the assumption that every organization which can execute ALGOL programs on a machine will have made those extensions to the language dictated by its specific needs.

Such extensions were also introduced for the MC-translator. They fall outside the scope of official language, and are, therefore, somewhat less definite. If the organization of the MC-translator is changed or extended in the future, we may expect the changes to take place in this field.

The solution which has been chosen shows considerable analogy with the way in which the standard functions are incorporated. There, special identifiers were introduced in order to indicate a function (with a result to be used as a term in an expression). Here, special identifiers are introduced in order to represent somewhat less standard actions. In the text in which such a standard action occurs, the latter plays the role of a complete, self-contained statement. We now mention two of these.

NLCR   : New Line Carriage Return

print (E) : Print the value of the expression E.

As long as the statement NLCR is not executed, successive print statements type the numbers one after the other on the same line. After the statement NLCR, the next number to be typed is typed at the beginning of the following line. We shall illustrate the use of these statements by a few examples.

Let us consider our example of the complex multiplication. We shall write a program that goes on multiplying ad infinitum, but types out, after each thousand multiplications, the deviation of the square of the modulus from unity. These differences are to be typed out one below the other.

```
begin   real x, y, u; integer k;
        x:= 5/13; y := 12/13;
BB:     for k := 1 step 1 until 1000 do
        begin   u := 0.6 × x − 0.8 × y;
                y := 0.8 × x + 0.6 × y;
                x := u
        end;
        NLCR; print (x × x + y × y − 1); goto BB
end
```

The following example produces a table of sinh(x) and cosh(x) for x = 1(.01)2. Each line of the table consists of three numbers, the argument and the corresponding sinh and cosh. One should note that the final boundary in the **for** statement is chosen somewhat larger than the desired last value of the argument since the controlled variable is of type **real**. In this way we guarantee that the function is calculated for x = 2, but not for x = 2.01.

```
begin   real x;
        for x := 1 step 0.01 until 2.001 do
        begin   NLCR; print (x);
                print (0.5 × (exp(x) − exp ( − x)));
                print (0.5 × (exp (x) + exp ( − x)))
        end
end
```

The above program is not really neat, since we cannot guarantee that the increment in the **for** statement will be exactly represented. If this is indeed not so, at the end of the table, the argument will be in error by approximately a hundred times the original discrepancy. In the following version this inelegance is removed. Further, we have somewhat reduced the amount of computation to be done, the evaluation of the exponential function being relatively laborious. (To complete the picture, we must state that the speed of the X1 is such that the reduction of the amount of computational work does not increase the overall speed of this program. The X1 is such a fast computer that the speed of the typewriter, which will type continuously, determines the total time required for the execution of the program in the above version.)

```
begin   integer k; real x;
        for k := 100 step 1 until 200 do
        begin   NLCR; print (k/100); x := 0.5 × exp (k / 100);
                print (x − .25/x);
                print (x + .25/x)
        end
end
```

12. Comments

An ALGOL program can be made more readable by the insertion of explanatory remarks at salient points. These comments are only intended for the human reader, and must be ignored by the translator. In order that the translator can detect which portions of the text, being commentary, should be ignored and where the actual program begins again, comment insertion is governed by certain rules. There are two kinds of comment.

The first form of comment is introduced by the special symbol 'comment'. After this symbol, all the following symbols up to and including the next semicolon are regarded as being a commentary. In other words for this sort of comment, which may not include a semicolon, the symbol **comment** functions as an opening bracket and the semicolon as a closing bracket. Officially, this form of comment is permitted in ALGOL 60 only after a semicolon or after the symbol **begin**; the MC-translator permits it everywhere.

The second form of comment may be given after the symbol 'end'. After this symbol all symbols are regarded as part of the comment up to (but not including) the first semicolon, **end** or **else**. For the MC-translator there are two additional restrictions here. First, this sequence of symbols which are to be ignored may not include the symbols **begin**, **comment**, and the so-called string quotes ' ⋠ ' and ' ⋡ '. Secondly, this form of comment is not permitted after the **end** of the all-embracing pair of statement brackets, that is to say, at the end of a program. This form of comment is usually employed in order to indicate to which **begin** the **end** in question corresponds, a facility which may be of particular importance when the correspondence can no longer be clearly indicated by means of a well-chosen lay-out.

13. Arrays

The power of expression of ALGOL 60 is considerably increased by the introduction of the concept 'array'. The simplest example of an array is a vector, i.e. a sequence of subscripted variables. Each array is referred to by means of its own identifier; if one wishes to refer to an individual array element then one specifies the corresponding value of the subscript in square brackets after the array identifier. A subscript must always run through a sequence of consecutive whole numbers, the choice of the minimum and maximum values (lower bound and upper bound respectively) being left entirely to the programmer.

Before we can make use of the chosen array identifier, we must have announced this in advance by means of a so-called 'array declaration'. Furthermore, the **array** declaration contains a specification of the type (**real** or **integer**) of the individual elements, as well as the upper and lower bounds of the subscripts. In an **array** declaration one separates the lower and upper bound from each other by a colon and encloses this bound pair in a pair of square brackets immediately following the array identifiers in question. An example will clarify this.

Suppose we wish to introduce four vectors or, as we prefer to call them, one-dimensional arrays. Three of these, to wit the arrays with the identifiers *Mozart*, *Bach* and *Brahms*, consist of elements of type **integer** and the fourth array, called *Beethoven*, has elements of the type **real**. (All the elements of any array must always be of the same type.) The arrays *Mozart* and *Bach* have each five elements numbered from 1 to 5, the arrays *Brahms* and *Beethoven* have each nine elements numbered from -4 up to and including $+4$. We can declare these with the help of two declarations, i.e. one for each type:

> 'integer array *Mozart, Bach* $[1:5]$, *Brahms* $[-4:+4]$;
> real array *Beethoven* $[-4:+4]$'

The most important rules for the formation of **array** declarations can be deduced from this example. All arrays of the same type may be (but do not have to be) treated in one and the same declaration. If they are of type **integer**, then the declaration begins with the symbols 'integer array', if they are of type **real**, then the declaration begins with the symbols 'real array'. (In the case of **real array**, one may omit the symbol **real**, in other words, if, in an **array** declaration, the type is omitted, the type **real** is understood.) This is followed by an identifier (or a number of identifiers, separated from each other by a comma), after which the subscript bounds are given between square brackets. These subscript bounds refer to the identifiers in the list immediately preceding them. If the last array of the type under consideration has been introduced, then the declaration is terminated by a semicolon, otherwise there is a comma which indicates that one or more arrays of the same type, but with their own subscript bounds, are to follow.

We have hereby introduced 28 array elements, some of which, for example, are: *Mozart* [*1*], *Mozart* [*2*], *Mozart* [*3*], *Mozart* [*4*], *Mozart* [*5*], *Bach* [*3*], *Brahms* [−2] and *Beethoven* [*4*]. A subscript value may not lie outside its corresponding bounds: the element *Beethoven* [*9*], for example, is undefined.

Apart from such vectors, one can also introduce arrays with more than one subscript. These are introduced in the **array** declaration by putting a comma after the upper bound of the first subscript instead of the square closing bracket; after this comma we give the bound pair for the next subscript, etc. The square closing bracket then follows the upper bound for the last subscript. To refer to an element of a two or more dimensional array, it is not enough, as in the case of a vector, to specify a single subscript, one now has to give all the subscript values in order, separated from each other by commas.

The following **array** declaration introduces three arrays with elements of type **real**. Of these two are two-dimensional and one is three-dimensional.

$$\text{'array } Rembrandt,\ Vermeer\ [-10:+10,\ 3:7],$$
$$le\ Corbusier\ [0:10,\ 0:7,\ 0:4]\text{'}$$

The first two arrays each contain $21 \times 5 = 105$ elements, the last contains $11 \times 8 \times 5 = 440$ elements. Hence one can refer to the elements *Rembrandt* [*8, 4*] and *le Corbusier* [*3, 3, 3*]; the element *Rembrandt* [*4, 8*] is again undefined, since one of the subscript values —the last—lies outside the corresponding bounds. The element *le Corbusier* [*5, 2*] is undefined, because the number of subscripts is not in agreement with the declaration.

Essentially, the subscript of a subscripted variable is an integer value. One may also write an expression between the square brackets, e.g. *Mozart* [$i \times i - 1$], and the value of such an expression may itself be of type **real**, e.g. *Bach* [*sin*(*x*) + *cos*(*pi* × *exp*(*y* + *yy*) − *7*)]. In such a case, the expression is rounded off to the nearest integer. The element *Beethoven* [*3.5*] is again undefined.

In ALGOL 60, the declarations of a program must precede the first statement; for the rest, their order is left to the programmer. The MC-translator, however, requires that all scalar quantities must be declared before the arrays are declared. In all examples which follow we shall, for understandable reasons, keep to this convention.

Now we shall consider an example in which we multiply a matrix A, consisting of 20 columns of six elements each, by a column vector B. The example is complete with the input and output of the data: we shall type out the six elements of the product vector. We assume that the elements of A are punched columnwise on the tape and that the elements of vector B follow on the last of A on the same tape. To enable a working ALGOL program to have access to numerical information punched out on a paper tape, the vocabulary of the MC-translator is extended by the special function 'read'. The value of this function is equal to the value of the next number on the tape. Obviously the tape must be inserted in the tape reader of the X1 before the program asks for numbers from the tape.

```
begin  integer i, j; real s; array A [1:6, 1:20], B [1:20];
       NLCR;
       for j := 1 step 1 until 20 do
          for i := 1 step 1 until 6 do A [i, j] := read;
       for i := 1 step 1 until 20 do B [i] := read;
       for i := 1 step 1 until 6 do
       begin  s := 0;
              for j := 1 step 1 until 20 do s := A [i, j] × B [j] + s;
              print(s)
       end
end
```

The program consists primarily of four statements, i.e. *NLCR*, followed by three **for** statements. From the first of these we see that the statement following a **for** clause may again be a **for** statement. For the last of these, in which the actual calculation is described, we needed the statement brackets **begin** and **end**. The form of this program was dictated by the order in which the numbers from the tape became available. If we had first had the vector B on the tape, and then the matrix A, but now punched row-wise, a much simpler program would have sufficed, e.g.:

```
begin  integer i, j; real s; array B [1 :20];
       NLCR;
       for j := 1 step 1 until 20 do B [j] := read;
       for i := 1 step 1 until 6 do
       begin  s := 0;
              for j := 1 step 1 until 20 do s := read × B [j] + s;
              print(s)
       end
end
```

14. Uniqueness of Identifiers

We have now encountered 'identifiers' in a number of different cases:

> scalar quantities
> labels
> special functions and standard actions
> arrays.

It is forbidden to use one and the same identifier in a given part of the program with two different meanings, even if, theoretically speaking, this would not cause any ambiguity, since the way in which an identifier is used in the text may be descriptive of the nature of the object it refers to. In no part of the program can two of the following four possible objects occur simultaneously:

> the scalar 'sin' (in expressions or to the left of ' := ')
> the label 'sin' (in a **goto** statement or to the left of ':')
> the function 'sin' (followed by '(')
> the array 'sin' (followed by '[').

This limitation, which is expressed shortly and cryptically by the principle 'the identifier identifies', is one of the corner stones of ALGOL 60. This rule also concerns identifiers for objects that have not yet been discussed (Booleans, switches and procedures).

15. Procedures

The example of the multiplication of a matrix by a vector was given as an illustration of the use of arrays. Furthermore, it shows the **for** statement in all its glory. It clearly showed that the **for** mechanism is not only a counting mechanism which ensures that a statement will be repeated a number of times, but that the repeated statement can also make fruitful use of the value of the 'controlled variable'. Again, this little program controls, among others, the execution of 120 multiplications, and it is, therefore, a striking illustration of the compactness of descriptions in ALGOL. **For** statements are not the only means of shortening program texts: at least as important is the extremely flexible form of abbreviation which is available to us in the form of what is called a 'procedure'.

Let us consider a program containing a variable named 'cosphi', which has to be modified at a great number of different points in the program. The modification can be described by the assignment statement:

$$\text{'}cosphi := 2 \times cosphi \times cosphi - 1\text{'}.$$

Instead of writing out this statement at every point where cosphi must be thus changed, we can give this operation a name. Once this has been done, we only need to mention this operation (by means of the chosen identifier) wherever this operation has to take place.

For this operation we choose an identifier which has no other meaning in this part of the program. Let it be the identifier 'DUB'. We declare this choice in a so-called 'procedure declaration'. In its simplest form, it consists of the special symbol '**procedure**', immediately followed by the identifier selected; by means of a semicolon this identifier is separated from the following statement, which is the one to be coupled to the identifier. (This is the end of the declaration. Since declarations are as a rule followed by other declarations or by a statement, a semicolon will follow the statement discussed.)

In our example, the procedure declaration would take the following form:

$$\text{'}\textbf{procedure } DUB; cosphi := 2 \times cosphi \times cosphi - 1\text{'}$$

42

From now on it is sufficient to write '*DUB*' everywhere in the text where this statement is to be executed. The identifier '*DUB*' then represents a complete statement, called 'a procedure statement', which must be separated from other statements by semicolons in the normal way.

In use, the procedure *DUB* does not differ from the standard operation *NLCR* already referred to. The only difference is that the identifier *NLCR* belongs to the primitive vocabulary of the MC-translator and may therefore be used without any preceding declaration. It is now also clear how the statement *NLCR*, which was previously introduced more or less as an extra, syntactically fits into ALGOL 60. When in use, it is a procedure statement just as any other. The function of a small number of procedures (including *NLCR*) may be assumed to be defined; furthermore, the programmer has the mechanism of the procedure declaration at his disposal to define new procedures as required.

We now examine the case in which two variables '*a*' and '*b*' must be interchanged at several points in the program. It is easy to see that this requires three statements; hence there is sufficient reason to regard this as a procedure. The fact that the procedure declaration gives its name to the 'first following statement' does not deter us, because we can make use of the accepted method of combining a number of statements into a single one, i.e. we enclose them by the statement brackets **begin** and **end**. Giving the procedure for interchanging a and b the name 'change', we have:

> '**procedure** *change*;
>   **begin real** s;
> $s := a; a := b; b := s$
> .**end**'.

(In this case **end**, the last symbol of the declaration, must be followed again by a semicolon.)

The observant reader will have noticed that in this procedure declaration we have enclosed more between the brackets **begin** and **end** than the three statements: these are preceded by a declaration of the auxiliary variable that we need for the process of interchanging. In this way we ensure that, at every subsequent execution of the procedure *statement* 'change', the variable s is temporarily introduced for the duration of the execution, in order to be able to carry out the interchange. This variable s, which is called 'a local variable' of the procedure, since it is declared inside the procedure, has no meaning outside it. But in order to be able to explain what is meant by 'inside' and 'outside', it is not enough to look at the procedure declaration itself, we must regard the procedure 'change' in its environment, i.e. in the program in which this declaration occurs.

16. Local Quantities

As has already been pointed out the declarations must appear at the beginning of the program. ALGOL 60 does not prescribe the order of the declarations themselves, but the MC-translator makes certain requirements here. We have already seen that scalars must be declared before arrays. Furthermore, the MC-translator requires that procedures must be the very last to be declared. A program, in which the procedure 'change' is declared and used, would look something like this:

```
begin real a, b, . . .;
      integer . . .;
      integer array s, . . . [. . . : . . .] . . .;
      real array . . .;
      procedure change;
      begin  real s;
            s := a; a := b; b := s
      end
      . . . ; change; . . .; change; . . .; s [. . . ] := . . .; change; . . .
end
```

The program begins with five declarations. The first declares, among others, the variables a and b, which are assumed to occur in the program. The second declares any integers which may occur. The order of the first and second declarations (both for scalars) may be the other way round. The third and fourth declarations which could also have been given in the reverse order, declare any possible arrays. Here the identifier s has deliberately been introduced as the identifier of an integer array. The fifth declaration is that of the procedure called '*change*'. The statement defining the function of the procedure (in this case the piece from the second **begin** up to and including the corresponding **end**) is called the 'procedure body'. If the procedure body contains declarations, these declarations are local to the procedure body. The concept 'local' has two aspects, one lexicographical and the other dynamic.

45

The section of the program for which a declaration is valid is given by a lexicographical rule: in principle it extends from the last preceding **begin** up to the corresponding **end**. Such a section of the program is called a 'block' (which will be discussed later). It follows that the whole program is a 'block', and that the declarations at the beginning of the program refer to the whole of the program. This is illustrated by the **real** declared variables *a* and *b*: everywhere in the program the identifiers *a* and *b* refer to these variables. The procedure body itself is also a block (what is called an 'inner block' of the program block). Declarations at the beginning of this block ('**real** *s*') have a meaning only inside this block. Should an identifier, declared here, already have a meaning in the enclosing block, then this 'outside' meaning is temporarily forgotten (in our example, this applies to the identifier s referring to an integer array). At the end of the inside block, the outside meaning is restored. (The use of the word 'temporarily' in the sentence above is based on the assumption that one reads the ALGOL program from beginning to end. In order to stress the lexicographical aspect, the word 'spatial' would perhaps be better.) Hence one can say that the range of a declaration stretches over the whole of the block in which it is declared, including its inner blocks (and inner-inner blocks, etc.), unless the identifier is used for another purpose in such an inner block. Alternatively, one might wish to answer the question: how does one find the meaning (i.e. the corresponding declaration) of an identifier used somewhere in the program? One examines the beginning of the smallest block in which the identifier is contained, and, if it is declared here, then that answers the question. If not, we go on to examine the beginning of the next lexicographically enclosing block, to see whether we find the declaration there, and so on. In our example, the consequence of the double use of the identifier *s* is that, inside the procedure body of 'change', we can no longer refer to the outside array s as well. If we had wanted to be able to do so, then we should have chosen another identifier for the auxiliary variable needed in '*change*'.

In order to show that the name s regains its original meaning as soon as the procedure declaration is finished, we have written the identifier s followed by [. . .], in the line that represents the statements of the program.

The dynamic aspect of the 'local' character of the declaration '**real** *s*' concerns the procedure statement ' . . .; change; . . .' which occurs three times in our example. During the execution of the program the (execution of the) procedure statements must be replaced by the (execution of the) corresponding procedure body. This implies that a new variable s is introduced, starting with an undefined value. In the course of the execution of the procedure, it receives a value (in this case the value of a), but this variable ceases to exist as soon as the procedure statement is finished, that is to say, its value is irrevocably lost. From the point of view of time, a local variable is, therefore, a variable with a limited life-span: successive 'reincarnations' of such a variable are entirely independent of each other.

The official ALGOL 60 report is painstakingly silent on the matter of really executing an ALGOL program with the help of an automatic computer; such down to earth matters as storage allocation are carefully avoided. We should like to indicate in a few words how the MC-translator reacts to the existence of local variables. For each procedure statement, i.e. each time a procedure is activated anew, the necessary storage reservation for the local quantities of this procedure is made. As soon as the activation of this procedure has come to an end, these reservations are cancelled and the memory locations in question are, as a rule, immediately used for other purposes.

Our procedure '*DUB*' was purely an abbreviation. In the procedure '*change*' the procedure mechanism was enriched by temporary introduction of auxiliary quantities. The next element, parameter substitution, will be explained with the aid of an extension of this simple example.

17. Formal Parameters

Let us consider a program in which a great number of variables occur and in which the values of pairs of variables have to be interchanged at a large number of points, and in contrast, however, to the previous example, not always the same pair. In ALGOL 60 we have the possibility of defining, by means of a procedure, a certain mechanism (in this case the mechanism of interchanging), without specifying in the declaration to which variables this mechanism shall be applied. Instead, this will now be given at each individual procedure statement. This mechanism consists of what is called a 'procedure with formal parameters'. Let us clarify this with the following example.

```
begin  real a, b, c, d, e, . . .;
       integer i, . . .;
       array s [2:12], . . .;
       procedure w2 (e, f); real e, f;
       begin real s;
             s := e; e := f; f := s
       end;
       . . .; w2 (a, b); . . .; w2 (d, c); i := 5; . . .; w2 (s[i], e); . . .
end
```

The procedure named 'w2' has two 'formal parameters'; in the declaration they have been given the names 'e' and 'f' respectively. In the lexicographical sense, these two identifiers are local to the procedure body. Being the names of formal parameters they have no meaning outside the procedure body; inside the procedure body they are used to identify the first and second (in general: the nth) formal parameter by virtue of their appearance in the first and second (in general: the nth) position of the list of identifiers that follows in brackets on the procedure identifier at the head of the procedure declaration. If the name chosen for a formal parameter already had a meaning outside the declaration, this outside meaning is 'dormant' in the range occupied by the procedure body and the outside meaning comes back into force after the procedure body has been executed.

The round closing bracket after the last formal parameter must be followed by a semicolon. At this point space is left for what are called the 'specifications'. Although the structure of a specification may be identical to the structure of a declaration (as in the above example), the specification can be recognized as such on account of the position in which it appears. The specification '**real** *e, f*' in the above example signifies that in the procedure body that follows the formal parameters '*e*' and '*f*', just introduced, will only be used in the way in which one is allowed to use declared **real** variables.

The dynamic implication of the concept of formal parameters differs fundamentally from that of local variables (such as **real** *s*). Now, the procedure statement consists not only of the procedure identifier, but it must be followed by a list of names (or expressions, see later) enclosed between brackets. When the procedure identifier is replaced by the corresponding procedure body, all formal parameters of the body must be replaced by the corresponding identifiers (or expressions) given in the procedure statement. Less pretentiously: the formal parameter acts as an 'open space' in the procedure body, which is filled in by the procedure statement.

In our example the effect of the procedure statement '*w2* (*a, b*)' is to interchange the values of the variables *a* and *b*, but in '*w2* (*s* [*i*], *e*)' the values of *s* [*i*] and *e* are interchanged. In the latter case the result will, therefore, also depend on the current value of *i*. In the procedure statements of our example, the variables *a, b, c, d, s* [*i*] and *e* are 'actual parameters'. An actual parameter specifies what has to be substituted for the corresponding formal parameter in the interpretation of the procedure statement.

In the declaration of the procedure *w2* the parameters *e* and *f* are specified, the local variable *s* is declared. Particularly for variables, however, the difference between specification and declaration is very marked; the declaration effects the temporary introduction of a new variable at the beginning of the procedure statement; the specification, on the other hand, concerns a formal parameter, which is coupled to the corresponding actual parameter, i.e. to something that already exists at the beginning of the procedure statement.

A minor difficulty can arise when the actual parameter is substituted for the formal one that corresponds to it. The procedure statement '*w2* (*d, c*)' gives rise to the execution of the three assignment statements

$$'s := d; d := c; c := s'$$

and here the interchange is described by correct ALGOL statements. In the same way, however, the statement '$w2$ (s [i], e)' would lead to

$$'s := s [i]; s [i] := e; e := s'$$

but this is no longer legitimate ALGOL, as the single identifier s is used in two different meanings in the same context. But this is not a real difficulty. It is caused by the double use of the same identifier s, but identifiers can be chosen at will: by renaming all quantities in an ALGOL program we can write down a completely equivalent program, in which no identifier is used with two different meanings. For instance, the local variable named 's' could have been baptized 's in $w2$'. The difficulty mentioned above then no longer arises. It is the duty of every translator for ALGOL 60 to remove from the ALGOL programs all apparent difficulties and ambiguities that could arise in the form of a 'clash of names' in the interpretation of the procedure statement; such renaming is one of the functions of the translator that is implicitly understood.

There is still another difficulty. Let us consider the—unusually short—procedure, declared by

'**procedure** Q (u, v); **real** u, v; $u := v \times v$'.

If a, b and c represent real variables, then possible procedure statements are:

'Q (a, b)'   meaning '$a := b \times b$'
'Q (b, 10)'   meaning '$b := 10 \times 10$'
'Q (c, $a + 1$)' meaning '$c := (a + 1) \times (a + 1)$' and *not* '$c := a + 1 \times a + 1$' which is usually equivalent to $2 \times a + 1$.

The official ALGOL report therefore states explicitly that in substituting an actual parameter for a formal one, the actual parameter must be enclosed within an extra pair of brackets: '( )', wherever syntactically possible. (Hence not to left of the becomes sign ': =', but it can never be needed there: in the case of the above procedure a would-be statement 'Q ($a + b$, 15)' is not allowed).

Now that we have discussed the formal parameter we can see how the standard operation '*print*(E)', mentioned above, fits into the language syntactically: it can be regarded as a one parameter procedure that is available without explicit declaration.

18. Function Procedures

Besides the procedure which can be used as a complete statement in itself, ALGOL 60 allows a somewhat different form of procedure, viz. a procedure which may be used within an expression. In order to distinguish between these two types of procedures, we shall call the latter a 'function procedure' and its use in an expression a 'function call'.

We have already encountered examples of function procedures, viz. the special functions that may be used without explicit declaration: 'read' is a function procedure without parameters, 'sin', 'cos', etc. are function procedures with one parameter. Statements in which they are used, such as

$$\text{'bibo} := read; \ Fidel := 7 - cos \ (2 \times bibo)'$$

illustrate that a function call, occurring at a point in an expression where a number is also syntactically admissable, represents a (numerical) value. As long as an expression contains only numbers and variables, the evaluation of the expression implies that the values of these 'primaries' are picked up in order from left to right and that the arithmetic operations are executed as soon as both operands have been fetched or formed. If a function call occurs in an expression, then we ask for the value of a primary 'in a complicated way'. The evaluation of the expression is held up for a while; then the function procedure is executed, and, when it is completed, it has produced (as a by-product) a value. Using this value the evaluation of the expression is continued. (We could not describe the effect of the function call as simply as that of the procedure statement: the body of a function procedure also consists of one statement, but in ALGOL 60 one cannot insert a statement somewhere in the middle of an expression.)

The declaration of a function procedure differs from that of the non-function procedure in two respects. In the first place, the symbol **'real'** or **'integer'** is added right at the beginning as an indication of the type of the value represented by the function call. In the second place, the procedure must indicate clearly where the value is formed that is to be delivered to the outside world as 'the value of the function call'. For this purpose the following convention was chosen. Inside the body an assignment must occur with the identifier of the function procedure to the left of a becomes sign. In illustration we give some examples, first a function procedure without parameters.

Suppose that the expression

$$\text{'}sqrt \ (x \times x + y \times y)\text{'}$$

occurs so often in a program that it is worthwhile to introduce an abbreviation for it. If we choose the name 'r' for this function of x and y —its value being equal to the length of the radius—then the relevant declarations are:

> **begin real** $x, y, \ldots$;
>   **real procedure** r; $r := sqrt \ (x \times x + y \times y)$;
>   . . . .
> **end**

As the procedure is one without parameters, there are no specifications; as the procedure body consists of a single assignment statement, we can do without the statement brackets **begin** and **end**. Should the apparently innocent assignment statement

$$\text{'}a := r + 8.134\text{'}$$

occur in the program itself (indicated above by the dotted line), then this implies the calculation of the square root of the sum of the squares of the values that the variables x and y have at that moment.

We give the following example, which we quote from *A Course of ALGOL 60 Programming*, written by P. Naur,* more as a test for the reader to see whether he has grasped the full implication of the function procedure, than as an example that deserves to be followed frequently. On the contrary! The function procedure, declared within the range of a variable W by the declaration,

> **'real procedure** *Sneaky* (z); **real** z;
>   **begin** *Sneaky* $:= z + (z - 2) \uparrow 2$;
> $W := z + 1$
>   **end'**

will, when it is used, for example, in the statement

$$\text{'}P := Sneaky \ (v - 1) + 2\text{'}$$

---

*A Course of ALGOL 60 *Programming, with special reference to the DASK ALGOL system.* Peter Naur (Regnecentralen, Copenhagen, Second Edition, 1961).

have the side-effect of changing the value of the variable W 'on the sly'. As a result, the effect of the two statements

$$`Pip := Sneaky\,(k) \times W'$$

and

$$`Pip := W \times Sneaky\,(k)'$$

is no longer the same. Needless to say, such 'sneaky' function procedures should only be used with the greatest possible caution.

Remark 1: The two above assignments to the variable Pip are only unambiguously defined providing the primaries of an expression are to be evaluated in order from left to right. Careful examination of the official report, however, shows that this order is not explicitly defined, and one can, therefore, defend the point of view that the above assignments are undefined. The MC-translator evaluates the primaries of an expression in order from left to right, and for this translator the above assignments are unambiguous.

Remark 2: Actually we have already met the construction of a function procedure that, besides taking on a value at the call, also effects other modifications, for the standard 'read' has the side effect of passing on to the next number on the tape.

As our next example, we give the function of two integers which is defined to be the smallest non-negative remainder that can arise on dividing the first by the second; further, this function procedure is equipped with an emergency exit in case the divider happens to be zero.

```
'integer procedure MOD (p, q, L); integer p, q; label L;
    begin    integer s;
             if q = 0 then goto L;
             s := p − p : q × q;
             if s < 0 then MOD := s + abs (q) else MOD := s
    end'
```

An example where this procedure is used in an expression would be

$$`\text{if } MOD\,(n \times (2 \times n + 1),\ TRIAL,\ ALARM) = 0 \text{ then} \ldots'.$$

Here n and TRIAL must be declared to be variables or procedures of type **integer** and somewhere there must be a statement labelled 'ALARM'; as soon as the condition is evaluated at a moment when the variable TRIAL equals zero, the **if** clause is left for good and the

C

computation is continued at the point indicated by the label '*ALARM*'. When a formal parameter is specified to be a label (as in the above case the last one is), the form of the corresponding actual parameter must be such that it could also occur, in the capacity of a so-called designational expression, after **goto**; other possibilities are a switch element and a conditional designational expression (for both, see later).

We can also construct (function) procedures to which procedure identifiers or array identifiers must be supplied as actual parameters at the call. For example

```
'procedure TABULATE (arg, ans, n, fun); integer n; array arg, ans;
            real procedure fun;
  begin     integer i;
            for i := 1 step 1 until n do ans [i] := fun (arg [i])
  end'
```

One can use the procedure *TABULATE* to compute the sequence of function values corresponding to a given sequence of arguments; if x and y are linear arrays with lower bound at most 1 and upper bound at least 10, then a possible procedure statement is

'*TABULATE* $(x, y, 10, sin)$'.

Here it is assumed that the element x[1] up to and including x[10] had well-defined values. The corresponding elements of y then become equal to the sine of these values.

The last example shows that the specifications only give partial information concerning the admissable actual parameters. Thus they do not specify the dimension of the arrays to which the first two actual parameters must refer, nor is it expressed that their subscript bounds must satisfy certain conditions. Moreover it is not stated that the last actual parameter must be the identifier of a function procedure with exactly one numerical argument. The specifications are given more for the benefit of the translator than for the benefit of the user.

19. The Value List

The procedures described thus far are correct—at least, we hope that they are—but they are not quite realistic. Returning to the last but one example, let us investigate the implications of the function call in

'$k := MOD\,(n \times (2 \times n + 1), m \times (m + 7) - 3, m \text{ is wrong})$'.

This call defines the formal parameters p and q by fairly complicated expressions; if we inspect the text of the procedure MOD, then we see that as a rule the value of p is needed twice and that of q three or four times. But in the execution of the statement given above, this implies that the first actual parameter is evaluated twice and the second one three or four times. Obviously it is not our intention to keep the machine occupied by repeated evaluation of the same expressions and in this respect the function procedure MOD is not realistic.

The difficulty can be overcome by introducing two extra local variables

```
'integer procedure MOD (p, q, L); integer p, q; label L;
begin   integer s, ploc, qloc;
        ploc := p; qloc := q;
        if qloc = 0 then goto L;
        s := ploc − ploc : qloc × qloc;
        if s < 0 then MOD := s + abs (qloc) else MOD := s
end'.
```

The need for such a 'recoding' arises so often that a special mechanism for abbreviation has been introduced for this purpose: the specifications are preceded by the symbol **value**, followed by a list of formal parameter identifiers. By inserting such a 'value list', we can now give a shorter form of the improved version of MOD, viz.

```
'integer procedure MOD (p, q, L); value p, q; integer p, q; label L;
begin   integer s;
        if q = 0 then goto L;
        s := p − p : q × q;
        if s < 0 then MOD := s + abs (q) else MOD := s
end'.
```

55

The effect of the value list can also be described as follows. For all formal parameters occurring in the value list, the corresponding actual parameter is calculated once on entry into the procedure body, and the values thus obtained are assigned to the formal parameter, which will subsequently be treated as a normal local variable of the body. We should like to stress that the introduction of the value list did not essentially enrich the expressive power of the language. We can describe the effect with the rest of ALGOL 60 as well. In the last definition the fact that we then need new identifiers (e.g. '*ploc*' and '*qloc*'), has been pushed somewhat into the background.

Besides scalar formal parameters, the value list may also contain formal parameters specified to represent array identifiers. If a formal parameter is specified to be an array, then the corresponding actual parameter may only be an array identifier referring to an array of the correct dimensions. If this formal parameter occurs in the value list, a local array is introduced with the same number of subscripts and the same subscript bounds as the corresponding actual array. Subsequently, the outside array is copied into the local one element by element. The presence of a formal array identifier in the value list may, therefore, cause a considerable amount of work when the procedure is called in. N.B.: For the MC-translator the maximum number of dimensions of a value array is five. We do not expect this somewhat curious restriction to have any serious consequences for the user.

We leave the verification of the following consequences to the reader. If a formal parameter, specified to represent a scalar, occurs in the procedure body to the left of the becomes sign of an assignment statement, then a number or an expression (such as '*15*', '*+ a*', '*b/c*' or '*(d)*' etc.) is not allowed to act as the corresponding actual parameter, except when the formal parameter in question occurs in the value list.

20. Bound Variables

We should like to draw the reader's attention to an ingenious way of using formal parameters not included in the value list. As far as we know it was first discovered by J. Jensen, and it is therefore called 'Jensen's Device'. In the first place, it is a good test to see whether one has grasped the full implications of the concept of the 'formal parameter'; in the second place, one is introduced to a way of ALGOL programming that has already proved to be extremely useful.

Two formal parameters play a role here, say i and t. The procedure assigns values to the formal parameter i and the actual parameter corresponding to i is, therefore, not a number or an expression, but a single variable. The other formal parameter t occurs in expressions only and the actual parameter corresponding to t may therefore be an expression; in particular, it may be an expression the value of which depends on the value of the variable corresponding to the formal parameter i. This means, however, that the procedure can treat the formal parameter t as a function of the independent variable i. Some examples may serve to illustrate this.

First, the function procedure which forms the sum of a certain number of terms in a series; in actual fact, this function procedure plays the role of the usual summation sign.

```
real procedure SIGMA (i, h, k, t); value k; integer i, h, k; real t;
begin   real s;
        s := 0;
        for i := h step 1 until k do s := t + s;
        SIGMA := s
end
```

We could have placed h in the value list but from the point of view of efficiency this serves no purpose as the initial value in the **step-until** element is only fetched once. This is in contrast to the final limit k, which must be compared to the controlled variable at every passage of the cycle. The function procedure SIGMA 'sums the term t for i running from h up to and including k in steps of 1'.

Thus the expression

$$SIGMA\,(n, 1, 10, H\,[n])$$

is equal to the sum of the array elements $H[1]$, $H[2]$, . . . $H[10]$. For, the substitution of names gives rise to the program:

```
begin real s;
        s := 0;
        for n := 1 step 1 until 10 do s := H [n] + s;
        SIGMA := s
end
```

and this compound statement obviously gives $SIGMA$ the required value.

With the assumption of suitable declarations

$$SIGMA\,(k, 1, 20, A\,[k, k])$$

represents the spur of the 20 by 20 matrix A and

$$SIGMA\,(t, 1, 20, A\,[r, t] \times B\,[t])$$

is the scalar product of the rth row (or column) of A and the vector B

The sum of all the elements of the matrix A is then

$$SIGMA\,(k, 1, 20, SIGMA\,(r, 1, 20, A\,[r, k])).$$

If one follows the semantic definition of the procedure statement and copies the procedure body but replaces all formal parameters by the corresponding actual ones, one will notice that, due to the special form of the last actual parameter, the 'transcription' again calls for the procedure $SIGMA$. The MC-translator accepts such 'nested' activations of one and the same procedure without further ado.

We could also have formulated the procedure body in another way, viz. 'recursively'; then the procedure itself is already used in its own declaration. Such constructions are also perfectly permissible for the MC-translator.

```
real procedure SIGMA (i, h, k, t); value h; integer i, h, k; real t;
begin    if k < h  then SIGMA := 0
                    else
         begin    i := h;
                  SIGMA := t + SIGMA (i, h + 1, k, t)
         end
end
```

In the last assignment statement the total sum is written as the first term increased by the sum of the remaining terms; one should note that we are not allowed to reverse the order of these two addenda. Here the term t represents the first term and actually gets this value as long as i has the initial value, but the activation of *SIGMA* can, and usually does, alter the value of i. Here we have a further example of the non-commutativity already encountered with 'Sneaky'. To be honest—and there is no point in being dishonest—we must point out that the execution of the function procedure *SIGMA* in its last form temporarily demands an amount of memory space that increases proportionally with the number of terms to be summed.

21. Blocks

The concept 'block' was mentioned in passing in the discussion of the procedure declaration; this is the last important element of the language which has to be dealt with. It concerns the macroscopic structure of an ALGOL program.

Actually we have encountered the statement bracket **begin** and **end** performing two different functions. In the first place we encountered it as a bracket pair to make a compound statement, viz. to see to it that the group of statements enclosed thereby acts syntactically as a single statement with respect to its environment. We encountered the compound statement for the first time after the **if** clause, next after the **for** clause and, finally, in the procedure declaration for the definition of what was to be regarded as the procedure body. In the last case, however, we saw that declarations could occur between the symbol **begin** and the first following statement, and that such declarations only applied to the piece of text up to the corresponding closing bracket **end**. A possible additional function of statement brackets is, therefore, to indicate, in the lexicographical sense, the range in which certain declarations apply; note that we have in fact already encountered this function for the all-embracing bracket pair that indicates where the program begins and where it ends.

Every compound statement in which one or more declarations occur between the first **begin** and the first following statement, is called a block; conversely, declarations are only allowed at the beginning of a block. This implies that a declaration always follows the symbol **begin** or another declaration (and is then separated from it by a semicolon).

Local to a block are:

(a) all identifiers declared at the beginning of the block;
(b) all labels, if any, labelling a constituent statement of the block;
(c) when the block is a procedure body, all formal parameters of the procedure.

The lexicographical consequences of an identifier being local are:

(a) that, outside the block, the object referred to by this identifier ceases to exist; and

(b) that, from inside the block, no reference can be made to an object to which the same identifier refers outside the block.

Labels are by definition local to the block of which the statement labelled by it is a constituent part, and, therefore, labels are inaccessible from outside this block. As a result it is impossible to enter a block from outside via a **goto** statement; the only way of entering a block is via its opening bracket **begin** and then one automatically passes the declarations pertaining to the block.

(In accordance with this the MC-translator regards each procedure body as a block, irrespective of the presence of local declarations. Likewise each **for** statement is regarded as a block since one is not allowed to enter its range from outside by means of a **goto** statement.)

Now that we have dealt with the concept of a block other than a procedure body, we can describe the effect of a procedure statement more rigorously. We shall illustrate this for the procedure 'change', our example from section 16, which was declared by

> '**procedure** *change*;
> > **begin real** s;
> > > $s := a; a := b; b := s$
> > **end**'

If the text of a program now contains the procedure statement '*change*', for example,

> 'S1; *change*; S2'

then the semantic definition of the procedure statement requires that the procedure statement should be replaced by the complete procedure body, declarations included, and the three statements above are dynamically equivalent to

> 'S1;
> **begin**   **real** s;
> > $s := a; a := b; b := s$
> **end**;
> S2'.

The effect of the procedure statement has thus been described in legitimate ALGOL 60 by making use of an inner block.

There is a certain case in which one very definitely needs the concept of a block, viz. as soon as one has to operate on arrays the subscript bounds of which are not known beforehand. In our examples of **array** declarations the bounds have always been (signed or unsigned) whole numbers. For the MC-translator this is the only permissible form of subscript bounds in the **array** declarations of the outermost block, i.e. in the main program. In inner blocks, however, the subscript bounds may be arbitrary expressions dependent on variables, provided these variables have well defined values at the moment of entry into the block. The subscript bounds are then evaluated once and these values remain valid for this activation of the block, even if one of the variables that was relevant in the evaluation of the subscript bounds changes in value during the course of the activation of the block.

Suppose that we have to make a program operating on two vectors A and B. The values of the elements of these vectors are punched on a tape; first the elements of A and then the elements of B. As the length of the vectors can vary, each vector is preceded by its length on the tape, i.e. by its number of elements. The structure of the program can then be of the following form:

> **begin integer** *length A, length B, k*;
>   'and all other declarations but not those pertaining to the one-
>   dimensional arrays A and B'
>   *length A* := *read*;
>   **begin array** *A* [*1* : *length A*];
>   **for** *k* := *1* **step** *1* **until** *length A* **do** *A* [*k*] := *read*;
>   *length B* := *read*;
>   **begin array** *B* [*1* : *length B*];
>   **for** *k* := *1* **step** *1* **until** *length B* **do** *B* [*k*] := *read*;
>   'and now the actual program is written in this
>   inner-inner-block'
>   **end**
>   **end**
> **end**

22. Dynamic Arrays

In the **array** declarations of the outermost block the subscript bounds cannot depend on any variables; they are therefore constants and the MC-translator accepts signed or unsigned whole numbers here. In the **array** declarations of inner blocks arbitrary expressions are permitted: if the evaluation of such an expression leads to a result of type **real,** this is rounded off to the nearest integer in the usual way. The rule that the lower bound of any subscript may not exceed the corresponding upper bound (after rounding off when necessary) also applies here.

At the beginning of an inner block declarations of scalars and arrays can be preceded by the extra symbol 'own' (at the beginning of the outermost block this would be pointless). The result is that the values of these variables are not lost on leaving the block, as in the case of ordinary local variables. They are preserved and become available again at the first re-entry into the block. This concept was only partly incorporated in the MC-translator. In the first place, only whole numbers are permitted as subscript bounds for **own** declared arrays (in the same way as for arrays that are declared in the outside block). In the second place, only one value is retained at a time for each **own** declared variable (scalar or array element); this is not in accordance with the official rules of ALGOL 60 as soon as a procedure, in which **own** declared variables occur, is used recursively.

23. Conditional Expressions

Besides the conditional statement ALGOL 60 allows the so-called 'conditional expression'. Here the question whether a condition is satisfied or not does not determine the choice between two alternative statements, but between two alternative expressions. The whole unit plays the role of an expression.

The most important difference from the conditional statement is that in the conditional expression **else** is obligatory. (This follows from the fact that in ALGOL 60 an 'empty expression' has no meaning, this in contrast to the empty statement, viz. 'do nothing and go on'.)

For the conditional expression the analogous rule holds that the expression between **then** and **else** may not itself be a conditional expression. One can always satisfy this condition by inserting brackets, but here of course one must use the expression brackets '(' and ')'.

In illustration we will again make the variable MAX equal to the greatest of three variables a, b and c. We shall use the minimum number of brackets.

'MAX := **if** $a < b$ **then** (**if** $b < c$ **then** c **else** b)
     else if $a < c$ **then** c **else** a'.

However, we advise everybody who works with conditional expressions not to economize on the number of brackets. Thus one may write

'y := **if** $x < 0$ **then** $- x$ **else** x'

instead of

'y := $abs(x)$'

but for

'y := $abs(x) + 1$'

one must write

'y := (**if** $x < 0$ **then** $- x$ **else** x) $+ 1$'

because omission of the brackets would have resulted in

'y := **if** $x < 0$ **then** $(- x)$ **else** $(x + 1)$'.

Here again it does not seem wise to rely too strongly on the priority rules.

24. Logical Variables

Let us consider a program section in which two variables, say a and b, do not change in value. If a certain function of these variables, say a/b, occurs regularly in this program section, then we can make the program simpler. At the beginning of the block in question we declare a new auxiliary variable, say qab, by means of

'real *qab*'

and insert the assignment statement

'*qab* := *a*/*b*'

as soon as the variables a and b have the desired values. From this point onwards (and as long as the variables a and b do not change in value), we can replace the (sub-)expression '*a/b*' by the simple variable '*qab*', wherever it occurs. (Naturally, the quotient '*a/b*' is a rather simple expression; the more complicated such an expression is, the more effective the abbreviation.) This abbreviation is one of the essential functions of the assignment statement. Its other essential function is that after a and/or b have changed in value, the quotient of the original values remains available, viz. the value of *qab*.

Now suppose that, instead of an arithmetic expression, what we have called a condition occurs repeatedly in such a piece of program in which a and b do not change in value, for example the relation

'$a \uparrow 3 < b \uparrow 5$'.

Every time this condition is required (for example between the symbols **if** and **then** in a conditional statement or expression) this involves the computation of a third and fifth power. Naturally it is much more attractive to determine once and for all whether this condition is satisfied or not, as soon as the values of a and b are known. In order to retain the answer to this question, a third type of variable, what is called the 'logical variable' has been introduced into ALGOL 60. If we now wish to introduce the analogous abbreviation, we declare, at the

65

beginning of the block, a new logical variable, say *vab*, by means of the declaration

'**Boolean** *vab*'

and insert the assignment statement

'*vab* := $a \uparrow 3 < b \uparrow 5$'

as soon as the variables *a* and *b* have the desired values. From this point onwards (and as long as a and b do not change in value) we can replace the condition by the simple logical variable '*vab*'; we then write

'**if** *vab* **then** . . .'.

In this way we ensure that the machine does not raise the same numbers to the same powers repeatedly.

In the declaration for the logical variable we encountered a new symbol, viz. the symbol '**Boolean**'; the MC-translator accepts yet another representation of this symbol, viz. '**boolean**', a version which is somewhat easier to produce on our Flexowriter. (This symbol begins with a capital letter, because logical variables are named after George Boole, author of 'An Investigation of the Laws of Thought, on which are Founded the Mathematical Theories of Logic and Probabilities', first published in 1853.) From now onwards we shall write it with a small letter.

If the identifier of a **boolean** variable occurs at the left-hand side of a becomes sign, there must be a so-called 'logical expression' at the right-hand side. We have just seen an example of a logical expression in the assignment to '*vab*'. Earlier examples are to be found in the **if** clauses. ALGOL 60 has a wide range for the formation of more complicated logical expressions. For full details we refer the reader to section 3.4. of the official Report.

One further remark about the value of logical expressions or variables. In contrast to a numerical value, which may in principle range from minus infinity to plus infinity, a logical variable can only take one of two values, a relation being satisfied or not. To represent a numerical value we have at our disposal a certain number of 'primitive characters', viz. the ten decimal digits and the decimal point. For the representation of the two logical values we need two separate symbols; they are '**true**' and '**false**'.

Without going into details, we should like to show the reader some examples. The simplest logical expressions are the two logical constants 'true' and 'false'. (In the same sense as we can regard '*13.7*' as a trivial example of an arithmetic expression.) The next way of producing a logical value is by compaiing two arithmetic expressions in a so-called relation, e.g.

$$'x > y', 'a + b = c', 'sin(x) < .5',$$
$$'gin \neq whiskey', 'x \leq 0' \text{ or } 'y \geq 5 \times z'.$$

Besides these six relational operators, ALGOL 60 includes a number of logical operators, forming a logical value from one or two logical values.

The logical operator ' $\wedge$ ' (read as 'and') connects two logical values; the result only takes on the value **true** if both operands have this value, otherwise its value is **false**. Thus the condition

$$'0 < x \wedge x \leq 1'$$

is satisfied only if x lies in the range $0 < x \leq 1$.

The condition that x should lie outside this range can be expressed with the aid of the logical operator ' $\vee$ ' (read as 'or'). This can also connect two logical values, the result has the value **true** if at least one of the operands has this value, otherwise it has the value **false**. The condition that x should lie outside the range $0 < x \leq 1$, is therefore given by the logical expression

$$'x \leq 0 \vee x > 1'.$$

We could also have expressed this using the negation operator '$\neg$' (read as 'not'), which operates on a single logical value. The condition that x lies outside the range $0 < x \leq 1$, i.e. that it is not inside the range, can alternatively be written as

$$'\neg (0 < x \wedge x \leq 1)'.$$

25. Switch Declarations

In passing we have mentioned the switch; this is the last type of object, which occurs in ALGOL 60. A switch is nothing but a one-dimensional array, the elements of which are not numbers, but destinations (in the simplest case, labels). There is no question of mentioning subscript bounds, because the convention is that the elements are numbered starting at one. The upper bound is given implicitly, due to the fact that the switch declaration ends with a list of the successive elements.

The switch declaration consists of the symbol 'switch', followed by the identifier chosen for this switch, then—alas!—the becomes sign ':= ' and, finally, the list of destinations, separated from each other by a comma.

If in a certain block the identifiers AA, BB, CC and DD are labels and the identifiers i and k refer to integers, say, then the following switch declaration could occur at the beginning of the block.

'switch $SWITCH := AA, BB,$ if $i = k$
then CC else DD, $SWITCH$ [abs (i–k)]'.

If somewhere in the block we have

'goto $SWITCH$ [E]',

then the effect of this **goto** statement depends on the value of the expression E. (In the following we assume that the value of the expression E is of type **integer**; if it were of type **real**, then its occurrence in a subscript position would imply the usual rounding off.) The effect of this **goto** statement is only defined for E = 1, 2, 3 or 4. (This holds for the MC-translator; in official ALGOL the effect of the above **goto** statement is that of a dummy statement for all other values of E.) If E = 1, then the effect is that of

'goto AA',

if E = 2, that of

'goto BB',

if E = 3, that of

'goto if $i = k$ then CC else DD'

68

which—see section 3.5. 'Designational expressions' of the official Report—in its turn is equivalent to

'**if** $i = k$ **then goto** CC **else goto** DD'.

Finally, if i = 4, then the effect is that of

'**goto** $SWITCH\,[abs\,(i - k)]$';

what happens if it so happens that abs $(i - k) = 4$?

For further details we refer the reader to section 5.3. 'Switch Declarations' of the official Report. We should like to add that the restriction mentioned in 5.3.5. does not hold for the MC-translator.

26. The MC-Translator

For the sake of completeness we now give a list of special properties of the MC-translator.

(1) Only signed or unsigned whole numbers are admitted as subscript bounds in those array declarations that are either placed in the outermost block or preceded by the symbol **own**.

(2) Procedures in which declarations marked 'own' occur do not function in full accordance with the official Report when used recursively.

(3) In the declaration of function procedure the MC-translator makes no distinction between 'real' and 'integer' as opening symbol: the answer is a copy of the intermediate result—as produced by the arithmetic of the procedure—that is assigned to the procedure identifier.

(4) Declarations at the beginning of a block and specifications in the **procedure** heading must be given in the following order:
    (1) scalars
    (2) arrays
    (3) destinations
    (4) procedures.

(5) Only the first nine symbols of an identifier are taken into account.

(6) Labels beginning with a digit are not admitted.

(7) The following rules hold for numbers occurring in the text of an ALGOL program:

The number zero is always regarded as being of type **integer**, also when a decimal point is given or when there is an exponent following the numerical part $= 0$.

A number that, according to the rules, should be of type **integer**, as the decimal point and exponent are absent, is transferred to type **real** when its absolute value exceeds 67108863.

The absolute value of the decimal exponent may not exceed 600.

(8) The maximum number of subscripts for an array in the value list is five.

(9) In the **procedure** declaration the MC-translator demands a specification for every formal parameter.

70

(10) When a formal parameter is specified 'real', a corresponding actual parameter of type **integer** is allowed and vice versa. (This does not necessarily need to hold for library procedures; special restrictions for library procedures will always be mentioned explicitly.)

(11) The value of the special function 'abs' is of the same type as the actual parameter supplied to it.

(12) In ALGOL 60 a function procedure may be called, not only as part of an expression, but also as a statement all by itself. The value of the function procedure is then of no interest and is discarded. For the MC-translator this is not allowed for the special functions named earlier. (Thus one is not allowed to skip three numbers from the tape by:

'read; *read*; *read'*.)

(13) The primaries of an expression are calculated in order from left to right.

(14) A block may not be enclosed lexicographically by more than 30 blocks. (In this connection **for** statements and procedure bodies count as new blocks.)

(15) On entering a procedure body, parameters in the value list are evaluated in the order of specification. (This is of importance when the evaluation of one actual parameter has a bearing on the value of another one.)

(16) The MC-translator also accepts the symbol '**boolean**' for the symbol '**Boolean**', likewise also '**goto**' for '**go to**'.

(17) In the text typed out by the Flexowriter consecutive symbols constructed by underlining must be separated from each other by one or more blanks (or Tab) or by the passage from one line to the next.

(18) The symbols to be skipped after '**end**' should be restricted to letters, digits, the point and the comma.

(19) The statement following a **for** clause may not only change the value of the controlled variable, but may also change the controlled variable itself (viz. when this is a subscripted variable). However, one should avoid calling function procedures that 'sneakily' change the value of the controlled variable or the controlled variable itself, in the expressions occurring in the list elements (i.e. between **for** and **do**).

(20) After the last **end** of the program the MC-translator does not accept symbols that are to be skipped.

(21) The restrictions named in section 5.3.5. and section 4.6.5. of the official Report do not apply to the MC-translator.

(22) Restriction 4.7.6. of the official Report does not hold for the MC-translator. On insertion of the procedure body as result of a procedure statement non-locals of the procedure retain the meaning they had in the **procedure** declaration.

(23) Only the comma is allowed as parameter separator.

27. Special Input-Output Procedures

When using the MC-translator the programmer has the following procedures at his disposal without declaration:

'*read*'   is a function procedure the value of which is equal to the next number on the tape. The type of this function depends on the number read from the tape. This procedure may only be called provided that the tape in question is inserted in the tape reader of the machine.

The numbers on the tape are punched according to the convention of ALGOL 60. Separation between successive numbers can be achieved in a variety of ways, e.g. by putting only signed numbers on the tape. (The sign of the next number then marks the end of the previous one.)

'*stop*'   is a procedure that stops the X1, for example to give the operator the opportunity of putting a new tape into the tape reader, or of setting the console switches (see '*XEEN*' below). By pressing one of the keys of the console (BNA = Begin Next Address) the computation is continued.

'*print* (E)'   is a procedure that types out the value of the expression E on the typewriter. If the expression is of type **integer**, then it prints a signed whole number, non-significant zeros being replaced by spaces. Otherwise the value of E is printed in floating decimal form. The maximum number of numbers to be printed on one and the same line is 7.

'*TAB*'   is a procedure which gives a tabulation with the effect that a column is skipped.

'*NLCR*'   is a procedure 'New Line Carriage Return'.

'*XEEN* (E)'   is an integer procedure which must be supplied with an integer argument. Its result is a collation (logical multiplication) of the binary representation of the value of E and the so-called 'console-word', i.e. a set of 27 binary switches on the console of the X1. This function enables us to write ALGOL programs for our X1-machine that can be influenced during run time via the console.

73

APPENDIX

Report on the Algorithmic Language ALGOL 60

by

J. W. Backus, F. L. Bauer, J. Green, C. Katz, J. McCarthy,
P. Naur (editor), A. J. Perlis, H. Rutishauser, K. Samelson,
B. Vauquois, J. H. Wegstein, A. van Wijngaarden, M. Woodger

Introduction

Background. After the publication[1,2] of a preliminary report on the algorithmic language ALGOL, as prepared at a conference in Zürich in 1958, much interest in the ALGOL language developed.

As a result of an informal meeting held at Mainz in November 1958, about forty interested persons from several European countries held an ALGOL implementation conference in Copenhagen in February 1959. A 'hardware group' was formed for working cooperatively right down to the level of the paper tape code. This conference also led to the publication by Regnecentralen, Copenhagen, of an ALGOL Bulletin, edited by Peter Naur, which served as a forum for further discussion. During the June 1959 ICIP Conference in Paris several meetings, both formal and informal ones, were held. These meetings revealed some misunderstandings as to the intent of the group which was primarily responsible for the formulation of the language, but at the same time made it clear that there exists a wide appreciation of the effort involved. As a result of the discussions it was decided to hold an international meeting in January 1960 for improving the ALGOL language and preparing a final report. At a European ALGOL Conference in Paris in November 1959 which was attended by about fifty people, seven European repre-

[1] Preliminary report — International Algebraic Language, Comm. Assoc. Comp. Mach. 1, No. 12 (1958), 8.

[2] Report on the Algorithmic Language ALGOL by the ACM Committee on Programming Languages and the GAMM Committee on Programming, edited by A. J. Perlis and K. Samelson, Numerische Mathemetik Bd. 1, S. 41 — 60 (1959).

sentatives were selected to attend the January 1960 Conference, and they represent the following organisations: Association Française de Calcul, British Computer Society, Gesellschaft für Angewandte Mathematik und Mechanik, and Nederlands Rekenmachine Genootschap. The seven representatives held a final preparatory meeting at Mainz in December 1959.

Meanwhile, in the United States, anyone who wished to suggest changes or corrections to ALGOL was requested to send his comments to the ACM Communications where they were published. These comments then became the basis of consideration for changes in the ALGOL language. Both the SHARE and USE organisations established ALGOL working groups and both organisations were represented on the ACM Committee on Programming Languages. The ACM Committee met in Washington in November 1959 and considered all comments on ALGOL that had been sent to the ACM Communications. Also, seven representatives were selected to attend the January 1960 international conference. These seven representatives held a final preparatory meeting in Boston in December 1959.

January 1960 Conference. The thirteen representatives[1], from Denmark, England, France, Germany, Holland, Switzerland, and the United States, conferred in Paris from January 11 to 16, 1960.

Prior to this meeting a completely new draft report was worked out from the preliminary report and the recommendations of the preparatory meetings by Peter Naur and the Conference adopted this new form as the basis for its report. The Conference then proceeded to work for agreement on each item of the report. The present report represents the union of the committee's concepts and the intersection of its agreements.

As with the preliminary ALGOL report, three different levels of language are recognized, namely a Reference Language, a Publication Language and several Hardware Representations.

Reference Language

1. It is the working language of the committee.
2. It is the defining language.
3. The characters are determined by ease of mutual understanding

[1] William Turanski of the American group was killed by an automobile just prior to the January 1960 Conference.

and not by any computer limitations, coders notation, or pure mathematical notation.

4. It is the basic reference and guide for compiler builders.

5. It is the guide for all hardware representations.

6. It is the guide for transliterating from publication language to any locally appropriate hardware representations.

7. The main publications of the ALGOL language itself will use the reference representation.

Publication Language

1. The publication language admits variations of the reference language according to usage of printing and handwriting (e.g., subscripts, spaces, exponents, Greek letters).

2. It is used for stating and communicating processes.

3. The characters to be used may be different in different countries, but univocal correspondence with reference representation must be secured.

Hardware Representations

1. Each one of these is a condensation of the reference language enforced by the limited number of characters on standard input equipment.

2. Each one of these uses the character set of a particular computer and is the language accepted by a translator for that computer.

3. Each one of these must be accompanied by a special set of rules for transliterating from publication or reference language.

For transliteration between the reference language and a language suitable for publications, among others, the following rules are recommended.

Reference Language	Publication Language
Subscript brackets [ ]	Lowering of the line between the brackets and removal of the brackets.
Exponentiation ↑	Raising of the exponent.
Parentheses ( )	Any form of parentheses, brackets, braces.
Basis of ten $_{10}$	Raising of the ten and of the following integral number, inserting of the intended multiplication sign.

Description of the Reference Language

Was sich überhaupt sagen läßt, läßt sich
klar sagen; und wovon man nicht reden
kann, darüber muß man schweigen.
                    LUDWIG WITTGENSTEIN

1. Structure of the language

As stated in the introduction, the algorithmic language has three different
kinds of representations—reference, hardware, and publication—and
the development described in the sequel is in terms of the reference
representation. This means that all objects defined within the language are represented by a given set of symbols—and it is only in the
choice of symbols that the other two representations may differ. Structure and content must be the same for all representations.

The purpose of the algorithmic language is to describe computational
processes. The basic concept used for the description of calculating rules
is the well known arithmetic expression containing as constituents
numbers, variables, and functions. From such expressions are com-
pounded, by applying rules of arithmetic composition, self-contained
units of the language—explicit formulae—called assignment statements.

To show the flow of computational processes, certain nonarithmetic
statements and statement clauses are added which may describe e.g.,
alternatives, or iterative repetitions of computing statements. Since it is
necessary for the function of these statements that one statement refers
to another, statements may be provided with labels. Sequences of statements may be combined into compound statements by insertion of
statement brackets.

Statements are supported by declarations which are not themselves
computing instructions, but inform the translator of the existence and
certain properties of objects appearing in statements, such as the class
of numbers taken on as values by a variable, the dimension of an array
of numbers or even the set of rules defining a function. Each declaration
is attached to and valid for one compound statement. A compound
statement which includes declarations is called a block.

A program is a self-contained compound statement, i.e. a compound
statement which is not contained within another compound statement

77

and which makes no use of other compound statements not contained within it.

In the sequel the syntax and semantics of the language will be given[1].

1.1. Formalism for syntactic description.

The syntax will be described with the aid of metalinguistic formulae[2]. Their interpretation is best explained by an example:

$$\langle a\ b \rangle ::= (\ |\ [\ |\ \langle a\ b \rangle\ (\ |\ \langle a\ b \rangle\ \langle d \rangle$$

Sequences of characters enclosed in the bracket $\langle\ \rangle$ represent metalinguistic variables whose values are sequences of symbols. The marks $::=$ and $|$ (the latter with the meaning of **or**) are metalinguistic connectives. Any mark in a formula, which is not a variable or a connective, denotes itself (or the class of marks which are similar to it). Juxtaposition of marks and/or variables in a formula signifies juxtaposition of the sequences denoted. Thus the formula above gives a recursive rule for the formation of values of the variable $\langle a\ b \rangle$. It indicates that $\langle a\ b \rangle$ may have the value (or [or that given some legitimate value of $\langle a\ b \rangle$, another may be formed by following it with the character (or by following it with some value of the variable $\langle d \rangle$. If the values of $\langle d \rangle$ are the decimal digits, some values of $\langle a\ b \rangle$ are:

```
[((((1(37(
(12345(
(((
[86
```

In order to facilitate the study the symbols used for distinguishing the metalinguistic variables (i.e. the sequences of characters appearing within the brackets $\langle\ \rangle$ as a b in the above example) have been chosen to be words describing approximately the nature of the corresponding variable. Where words which have appeared in this manner are used elsewhere in the text they will refer to the corresponding syntactic

[1] Whenever the precision of arithmetic is stated as being in general not specified, or the outcome of a certain process is said to be undefined, this is to be interpreted in the sense that a program only fully defines a computational process if the accompanying information specifies the precision assumed, the kind of arithmetic assumed, and the course of action to be taken in all such cases as may occur during the execution of the computation.

[2] Cf. J. W. BACKUS, The syntax and semantics of the proposed international algebraic language of the Zürich ACM-GAMM conference. ICIP Paris. June 1959.

definition. In addition some formulae have been given in more than one place.

Definition:
⟨empty⟩:: =
(i.e. the null string of symbols).

2. Basic symbols, identifiers, numbers, and strings.
Basic concepts

The reference language is built up from the following basic symbols:
⟨basic symbol⟩:: = ⟨letter⟩ | ⟨digit⟩ | ⟨logical value⟩ | ⟨delimiter⟩

2.1. Letters
⟨letter⟩ :: = $a|b|c|d|e|f|g|h|i|j|k|l|m|n|o|p|q|r|s|t|u|v|w|x|y|z|$
$A|B|C|D|E|F|G|H|I|J|K|L|M|N|O|P|Q|R|S|T|U|V|W|X|Y|Z$
This alphabet may arbitrarily be restricted, or extended with any other distinctive character (i.e. character not coinciding with any digit, logical value or delimiter).

Letters do not have individual meaning. They are used for forming identifiers and strings[1] (cf sections 2.4. Identifiers, 2.6. Strings).

2.2.1. Digits
⟨digit⟩ :: = $0|1|2|3|4|5|6|7|8|9$
Digits are used for forming numbers, identifiers, and strings.

2.2.2. Logical values
⟨logical value⟩ :: = **true**|**false**
The logical values have a fixed obvious meaning.

2.3. Delimiters
⟨delimiter⟩ :: = ⟨operator⟩ | ⟨separator⟩ | ⟨bracket⟩ | ⟨declarator⟩ |
    ⟨specificator⟩
⟨operator⟩ :: = ⟨arithmetic operator⟩ | ⟨relational operator⟩ | ⟨logical
    operator⟩ | ⟨sequential operator⟩
⟨arithmetic operator⟩ :: = $+ | - | \times | / | \div | \uparrow$
⟨relational operator⟩ :: = $< | \leq | = | \geq | > | \neq$
⟨logical operator⟩ :: = $\equiv | \supset | \vee | \wedge | \neg$

---

[1] It should be particularly noted that throughout the reference language under-lining (*for typographical reasons synonymously bold type. Publishers remark*) is used for defining independent basic symbols (see sections 2.2.2. and 2.3). These are understood to have no relation to the individual letters of which they are composed.

⟨sequential operator⟩ :: = **go to** |**if**|**then**|**else**|**for**|**do**[1]

⟨separator⟩ :: = , | . | $_{10}$ | : | ; | := | ⊔ | **step**|**until**|**while**|**comment**

⟨bracket⟩ :: = (|) | [|] | ' | ' | **begin**|**end**

⟨declarator⟩ :: = **own** | **Boolean** | **integer** | **real** | **array** | **switch** | **procedure**

⟨specificator⟩ :: = **string** | **label** | **value**

Delimiters have a fixed meaning which for the most part is obvious, or else will be given at the appropriate place in the sequel.

Typographical features such as blank space or change to a new line have no significance in the reference language. They may, however, be used freely for facilitating reading.

For the purpose of including text among the symbols of a program the following 'comment' conventions hold:

The sequence of basic symbols: is equivalent with

; **comment** ⟨any sequence not containing ;⟩;   ;

begin comment ⟨any sequence not containing ;⟩;   **begin**

end ⟨any sequence not containing **end** or ; or **else**⟩   **end**

By equivalence is here meant that any of the three symbols shown in the right hand column may, in any occurrence outside of strings, be replaced by any sequence of symbols of the structure shown in the same line of the left hand column without any effect on the action of the program.

2.4. Identifiers

2.4.1. Syntax.

⟨identifier⟩ :: = ⟨letter⟩|⟨identifier⟩⟨letter⟩|⟨identifier⟩⟨digit⟩

2.4.2. Examples   *q*

Soup

V 17 a

a 34 k T M N s

M A R I L Y N

2.4.3. Semantics. Identifiers have no inherent meaning, but serve for the identification of simple variables, arrays, labels, switches, and procedures. They may be chosen freely (cf. however section 3.2.4. Standard functions).

The same identifier cannot be used to denote two different quantities except when these quantities have disjoint scopes as defined by the declarations of the program (cf. section 2.7. Quantities, kinds and scopes and section 5. Declarations).

---

[1] **do** is used in for statements. It has no relation whatsoever to the *do* of the preliminary report, which is not included in ALGOL 60.

2.5. Numbers

2.5.1. Syntax.

$\langle$unsigned integer$\rangle$ :: $= \langle$digit$\rangle | \langle$unsigned integer$\rangle \langle$digit$\rangle$

$\langle$integer$\rangle$ :: $= \langle$unsigned integer$\rangle | +\langle$unsigned integer$\rangle | -\langle$unsigned integer$\rangle$

$\langle$decimal fraction$\rangle$ :: $= . \langle$unsigned integer$\rangle$

$\langle$exponent part$\rangle$ :: $= {}_{10}\langle$integer$\rangle$

$\langle$decimal number$\rangle$ :: $= \langle$unsigned integer$\rangle | \langle$decimal fraction$\rangle |$
$\langle$unsigned integer$\rangle \langle$decimal fraction$\rangle$

$\langle$unsigned number$\rangle$ :: $= \langle$decimal number$\rangle | \langle$exponent part$\rangle |$
$\langle$decimal number$\rangle \langle$exponent part$\rangle$

$\langle$number$\rangle$ :: $= \langle$unsigned number$\rangle | + \langle$unsigned number$\rangle | - \langle$unsigned number$\rangle$

2.5.2. Examples.

0	-200.084	$-.083_{10}-02$
177	$+07.43_{10}8$	$-_{10}7$
$.5384$	$9.34_{10}+10$	$_{10}-4$
$+0.7300$	$2_{10}-4$	$+_{10}+5$

2.5.3. Semantics. Decimal numbers have their conventional meaning. The exponent part is a scale factor expressed as an integral power of 10.

2.5.4. Types. Integers are of type **integer**. All other numbers are of type **real** (cf. section 5.1. Type declarations).

2.6. Strings

2.6.1. Syntax.

$\langle$proper string$\rangle$ :: $= \langle$any sequence of basic symbols not containing 'or'$\rangle | \langle$empty$\rangle$

$\langle$open string$\rangle$ :: $= \langle$proper string$\rangle | {}'\langle$open string$\rangle' | \langle$open string$\rangle \langle$open string$\rangle$

$\langle$string$\rangle$ :: $= {}'\langle$open string$\rangle'$

2.6.2. Examples.

$$'5k,, - {}'[[['\wedge = /:'T\ t'{}'$$

$$'..This \sqcup is \sqcup a \sqcup 'string'{}'$$

2.6.3. Semantics. In order to enable the language to handle arbitrary sequences of basic symbols the string quotes ' and ' are introduced. The symbol $\sqcup$ denotes a space. It has no significance outside strings.

Strings are used as actual parameters of procedures (cf. sections 3.2. Function designators and 4.7. Procedure statements).

2.7. Quantities, kinds and scopes

The following kinds of quantities are distinguished: simple variables, arrays, labels, switches, and procedures.

The scope of a quantity is the set of statements in which the declaration for the identifier associated with that quantity is valid, or, for labels, the set of statements which may have the statement in which the label occurs as their successor.

2.8. Values and types

A value is an ordered set of numbers (special case: a single number), an ordered set of logical values (special case: a single logical value), or a label.

Certain of the syntactic units are said to possess values. These values will in general change during the execution of the program. The values of expressions and their constituents are defined in section 3. The value of an array identifier is the ordered set of values of the corresponding array of subscripted variables (cf. section 3.1.4.1).

The various 'types' (**integer, real, Boolean**) basically denote properties of values. The types associated with syntactic units refer to the values of these units.

3. *Expressions*

In the language the primary constituents of the programs describing algorithmic processes are arithmetic, Boolean, and designational, expressions. Constituents of these expressions, except for certain delimiters, are logical values, numbers, variables, function designators, and elementary arithmetic, relational, logical, and sequential, operators. Since the syntactic definition of both variables and function designators contains expressions, the definition of expressions, and their constituents, is necessarily recursive.

⟨expression⟩ :: = ⟨arithmetic expression⟩ | ⟨Boolean expression⟩ |
  ⟨designational expression⟩

3.1. Variables

3.1.1. Syntax.
⟨variable identifier⟩ :: = ⟨identifier⟩
⟨simple variable⟩ :: = ⟨variable identifier⟩
⟨subscript expression⟩ :: = ⟨arithmetic expression⟩

⟨subscript list⟩ :: = ⟨subscript expression⟩ | ⟨subscript list⟩, ⟨sub-
    script expression⟩
⟨array identifier⟩ :: = ⟨identifier⟩
⟨subscripted variable⟩ :: = ⟨array identifier⟩ [⟨subscript list⟩]
⟨variable⟩ :: = ⟨simple variable⟩ | ⟨subscripted variable⟩

3.1.2. Examples.   *epsilon*
                          det A
                          a 17
                          Q [*7, 2*]
                          x [*sin* (*n* × *pi/2*), *Q* [*3, n, 4*]]

3.1.3. Semantics. A variable is a designation given to a single value. This
value may be used in expressions for forming other values and may be
changed at will by means of assignment statements (section 4.2). The
type of the value of a particular variable is defined in the declaration
for the variable itself (cf. section 5.1. Type declarations) or for the
corresponding array identifier (cf. section 5.2. Array declarations).
3.1.4. Subscripts. 3.1.4.1. Subscripted variables designate values which
are components of multidimensional arrays (cf. section 5.2. Array
declarations). Each arithmetic expression of the subscript list occupies
one subscript position of the subscripted variable, and is called a subscript. The complete list of subscripts is enclosed in the subscript brackets
[]. The array component referred to by a subscripted variable is specified
by the actual numerical value of its subscripts (cf. section 3.3. Arithmetic expressions).

3.1.4.2. Each subscript position acts like a variable of type **integer** and the
evaluation of the subscript is understood to be equivalent to an assignment to this fictitious variable (cf. section 4.2.4). The value of the
subscripted variable is defined only if the value of the subscript expression is within the subscript bounds of the array (cf. section 5.2.
Array declarations).

3.2. Function designators

3.2.1. Syntax.
⟨procedure identifier⟩ :: = ⟨identifier⟩
⟨actual parameter⟩ :: = ⟨string⟩ | ⟨expression⟩ | ⟨array identifier⟩ |
    ⟨switch identifier⟩ | ⟨procedure identifier⟩
⟨letter string⟩ :: = ⟨letter⟩ | ⟨letter string⟩ ⟨letter⟩
⟨parameter delimiter⟩ :: = ,|) ⟨letter string⟩ : (

⟨actual parameter list⟩ :: = ⟨actual parameter⟩ |
  ⟨actual parameter list⟩ ⟨parameter delimiter⟩ ⟨actual parameter⟩
⟨actual parameter part⟩ :: = ⟨empty⟩ | (⟨actual parameter list⟩)
⟨function designator⟩ :: = ⟨procedure identifier⟩ ⟨actual parameter
  part⟩

3.2.2. Examples. $sin(a - b)$
$$J(v + s, n)$$
$$R$$
$$S(s - 5)\,Temperature:(T)Pressure:(P)$$
$$Compile(':=')\,Stack:(Q)$$

3.2.3. Semantics. Function designators define single numerical or
logical values, which result through the application of given sets of rules
defined by a procedure declaration (cf. section 5.4. Procedure declarations) to fixed sets of actual parameters. The rules governing specification
of actual parameters are given in section 4.7. Procedure statements'
Not every procedure declaration defines the value of a function designator.

3.2.4. Standard functions. Certain identifiers should be reserved for the
standard functions of analysis, which will be expressed as procedures.
It is recommended that this reserved list should contain:

abs (E)   for the modulus (absolute value) of the value of the ex-
          pression E
sign (E)   for the sign of the value of E ($+ 1$ for E > 0, 0 for E $= 0$,
          -1 for E < 0)
sqrt (E)   for the square root of the value of E
sin (E)   for the sine of the value of E
cos (E)   for the cosine of the value of E
arctan(E) for the principal value of the arctangent of the value of E
ln (E)   for the natural logarithm of the value of E
exp (E)   for the exponential function of the value of E (e^E)
These functions are all understood to operate indifferently on arguments
both of type **real** and **integer**. They will all yield values of type **real**,
except for *sign* (E) which will have values of type **integer**. In a particular
representation these functions may be available without explicit declarations (cf. section 5. Declarations).

3.2.5. Transfer functions. It is understood that transfer functions between any pair of quantities and expressions may be defined. Among the

standard functions it is recommended that there be one, namely
  entier (E),
which 'transfers' an expression of real type to one of integer type, and
assigns to it the value which is the largest integer not greater than the
value of E.

3.3. Arithmetic expressions

3.3.1. Syntax. $\langle$ adding operator $\rangle$ :: $= + \mid -$
$\langle$ multiplying operator $\rangle$ :: $= \times \mid / \mid \div$
$\langle$ primary $\rangle$ :: $= \langle$ unsigned number $\rangle \mid \langle$ variable $\rangle \mid \langle$ function designator $\rangle \mid$
  ($\langle$ arithmetic expression $\rangle$)
$\langle$ factor $\rangle$ :: $= \langle$ primary $\rangle \mid \langle$ factor $\rangle \uparrow \langle$ primary $\rangle$
$\langle$ term $\rangle$ :: $= \langle$ factor $\rangle \mid \langle$ term $\rangle \langle$ multiplying operator $\rangle \langle$ factor $\rangle$
$\langle$ simple arithmetic expression $\rangle$ :: $= \langle$ term $\rangle \mid \langle$ adding operator $\rangle$
  $\langle$ term $\rangle \mid \langle$ simple arithmetic expression $\rangle \langle$ adding operator $\rangle \langle$ term $\rangle$
$\langle$ if clause $\rangle$ :: $=$ **if** $\langle$ Boolean expression $\rangle$ **then**
$\langle$ arithmetic expression $\rangle$ :: $= \langle$ simple arithmetic expression $\rangle \mid$
  $\langle$ if clause $\rangle$ $\langle$ simple arithmetic expression $\rangle$ **else** $\langle$ arithmetic expression $\rangle$

3.3.2. Examples.
  Primaries:
$7.394_{10} - 8$
sum
$w\,[i + 2,8]$
$cos(y + z \times 3)$
$(a - 3/y + vu \uparrow 8)$

  Factors:
omega
$sum \uparrow cos(y + z \times 3)$
$7.394_{10} - 8 \uparrow w\,[i + 2,8] \uparrow (a - 3/y + vu \uparrow 8)$

  Terms:
U
$omega \times sum \uparrow cos\,(y + z \times 3)/7.394_{10} - 8 \uparrow w\,[i + 2,8] \uparrow$
  $(a - 3/y + vu \uparrow 8)$

  Simple arithmetic expression:
$U - Yu + omega \times sum \uparrow cos(y + z \times 3)/7.394_{10} - 8 \uparrow w\,[i + 2, 8] \uparrow$
  $(a - 3/y + vu \uparrow 8)$

D

Arithmetic expressions:

$w \times u - Q(S + Cu) \uparrow 2$

if $q > 0$ **then** $S + 3 \times Q/A$ **else** $2 \times S + 3 \times q$

if $a < 0$ **then** $U + V$ **else if** $a \times b > 17$ **then** U/V **else if** $k \neq y$ **then** V/U
  else 0

$a \times \sin(omega \times t)$

$0.57_{10}12 \times a\,[N \times (N-1)/2, 0]$

$(A \times \arctan(y) + Z) \uparrow (7 + Q)$

if q **then** $n - 1$ **else** n

if $a < 0$ **then** A/B **else if** $b = 0$ **then** B/A **else** z

3.3.3. Semantics. An arithmetic expression is a rule for computing a numerical value. In case of simple arithmetic expressions this value is obtained by executing the indicated arithmetic operations on the actual numerical values of the primaries of the expression, as explained in detail in section 3.3.4. below. The actual numerical value of a primary is obvious in the case of numbers. For variables it is the current value (assigned last in the dynamic sense), and for function designators it is the value arising from the computing rules defining the procedure (cf. section 5.4. Procedure declarations) when applied to the current values of the procedure parameters given in the expression. Finally, for arithmetic expressions enclosed in parentheses the value must through a recursive analysis be expressed in terms of the values of primaries of the other three kinds.

In the more general arithmetic expressions, which include if clauses, one out of several simple arithmetic expressions is selected on the basis of the actual values of the Boolean expressions (cf. section 3.4. Boolean expressions). This selection is made as follows: The Boolean expressions of the if clauses are evaluated one by one in sequence from left to right until one having the value **true** is found. The value of the arithmetic expression is then the value of the first arithmetic expression following this Boolean (the largest arithmetic expression found in this position is understood). The construction:

  else ⟨simple arithmetic expression⟩

is equivalent to the construction:

  else if true then ⟨simple arithmetic expression⟩

3.3.4. Operators and types. Apart from the Boolean expressions of if clauses, the constituents of simple arithmetic expressions must be of types **real** or **integer** (cf. section 5.1. Type declarations). The meaning of the basic operators and the types of the expressions to which they lead are given by the following rules:

3.3.4.1. The operators $+$, $-$, and $\times$ have the conventional meaning (addition, subtraction, and multiplication). The type of the expression will be **integer** if both of the operands are of **integer** type, otherwise **real**.

3.3.4.2. The operations $\langle\text{term}\rangle / \langle\text{factor}\rangle$ and $\langle\text{term}\rangle \div \langle\text{factor}\rangle$ both denote division, to be understood as a multiplication of the term by the reciprocal of the factor with due regard to the rules of precedence (cf. section 3.3.5). Thus for example

$a/b \times 7/(p-q) \times v/s$

means

$((((a \times (b^{-1})) \times 7) \times ((p-q)^{-1})) \times v) \times (s^{-1})$

The operator $/$ is defined for all four combinations of types **real** and **integer** and will yield results of **real** type in any case. The operator $\div$ is defined only for two operands both of type **integer** and will yield a result of type **integer** defined as follows:

$a \div b = sign\,(a/b) \times entier\,(abs\,(a/b))$

(cf. sections 3.2.4 and 3.2.5).

3.3.4.3. The operation $\langle\text{factor}\rangle \uparrow \langle\text{primary}\rangle$ denotes exponentiation, where the factor is the base and the primary is the exponent. Thus for example

$2 \uparrow n \uparrow k$ means $(2^n)^k$

while

$2 \uparrow (n \uparrow m)$ means $2^{(nm)}$

Writing i for a number of **integer** type, r for a number of **real** type, and a for a number of either **integer** or **real** type, the result is given by the following rules:

$a \uparrow i$	If $i > 0$:	$a \times a \times \cdots \times a$ (i times), of the same type as a.
	If $i = 0$, if $a \neq 0$:	1, of the same type as a.
	if $a = 0$:	undefined.
	If $i < 0$, if $a \neq 0$:	$1/(a \times a \times \cdots \times a)$ (the denominator has $-i$ factors), of type **real**.
	if $a = 0$:	undefined.
$a \uparrow r$	If $a > 0$:	$\exp\,(r \times ln\,(a))$, of type **real**.
	If $a = 0$, if $r > 0$:	0.0, of type **real**.
	if $r \leq 0$:	undefined.
	If $a < 0$: always undefined.	

3.3.5. Precedence of operators. The sequence of operations within one expression is generally from left to right, with the following additional rules:

3.3.5.1. According to the syntax given in section 3.3.1 the following rules of precedence hold:

first: $\uparrow$
second: $\times / \div$
third: $+ \ -$

3.3.5.2. The expression between a left parenthesis and the matching right parenthesis is evaluated by itself and this value is used in subsequent calculations. Consequently the desired order of execution of operations within an expression can always be arranged by appropriate positioning of parentheses.

3.3.6. Arithmetics of **real** quantities. Numbers and variables of type **real** must be interpreted in the sense of numerical analysis, i.e. as entities defined inherently with only a finite accuracy. Similarly, the possibility of the occurrence of a finite deviation from the mathematically defined result in any arithmetic expression is explicitly understood. No exact arithmetic will be specified, however, and it is indeed understood that different hardware representations may evaluate arithmetic expressions differently. The control of the possible consequences of such differences must be carried out by the methods of numerical analysis. This control must be considered a part of the process to be described, and will therefore be expressed in terms of the language itself.

3.4. Boolean expressions

3.4.1. Syntax.

$\langle$relational operator$\rangle$ :: $= < \mid \leq \mid = \mid \geq \mid > \mid \neq$
$\langle$relation$\rangle$ :: $= \langle$arithmetic expression$\rangle$ $\langle$relational operator$\rangle$
    $\langle$arithmetic expression$\rangle$
$\langle$Boolean primary$\rangle$ :: $= \langle$logical value$\rangle$ $\mid \langle$variable$\rangle$ $\mid \langle$function
    designator$\rangle$ $\mid \langle$relation$\rangle$ $\mid (\langle$Boolean expression$\rangle)$
$\langle$Boolean secondary$\rangle$ :: $= \langle$Boolean primary$\rangle$ $\mid \neg \langle$Boolean primary$\rangle$
$\langle$Boolean factor$\rangle$ :: $= \langle$Boolean secondary$\rangle \mid$
    $\langle$Boolean factor$\rangle \wedge \langle$Boolean secondary$\rangle$
$\langle$Boolean term$\rangle$ :: $= \langle$Boolean factor$\rangle \mid \langle$Boolean term$\rangle \vee \langle$Boolean factor$\rangle$
$\langle$implication$\rangle$ :: $= \langle$Boolean term$\rangle \mid \langle$implication$\rangle \supset \langle$Boolean term$\rangle$

⟨simple Boolean⟩ :: = ⟨implication⟩ | ⟨simple Boolean⟩ ≡ ⟨implication⟩

⟨Boolean expression⟩ :: = ⟨simple Boolean⟩|
  ⟨if clause⟩ ⟨simple Boolean⟩ **else** ⟨Boolean expression⟩

3.4.2. Examples. $x = -2$

$$Y > V \lor z < q$$
$$a + b > -5 \land z - d > q \uparrow 2$$
$$p \land q \lor x \neq y$$
$$g \equiv \neg a \land b \land \neg c \lor d \lor e \supset \neg f$$

if $k < l$ **then** $s > w$ **else** $h \leq c$

if if if a **then** b **else** c **then** d **else** f **then** g **else** $h < k$

3.4.3. Semantics. A Boolean expression is a rule for computing a logical value. The principles of evaluation are entirely analogous to those given for arithmetic expressions in section 3.3.3.

3.4.4. Types. Variables and function designators entered as Boolean primaries must be declared **Boolean** (cf. section 5.1. Type declarations and section 5.4.4. Values of function designators).

3.4.5. The operators. Relations take on the value **true** whenever the corresponding relation is satisfied for the expressions involved, otherwise **false**.

The meaning of the logical operators − (not), ∧ (and), ∨ (or), ⊃ (implies), and ≡ (equivalent), is given by the following function table.

$b1$	false	false	true	true
$b2$	false	true	false	true
$-b1$	true	true	false	false
$b1 \land b2$	false	false	false	true
$b1 \lor b2$	false	true	true	true
$b1 \supset b2$	true	true	false	true
$b1 \equiv b2$	true	false	false	true

3.4.6. Precedence of operators. The sequence of operations within one expression is generally from left to right, with the following additional rules:

3.4.6.1. According to the syntax given in section 3.4.1. the following rules of precedence hold:

first: arithmetic expressions according to section 3.3.5.

second: $< \leq = \geq > \neq$

third: ¬
fourth: ∧
fifth: ∨
sixth: ⊃
seventh: ≡

3.4.6.2. The use of parentheses will be interpreted in the sense given in section 3.3.5.2

3.5. Designational expressions

3.5.1. Syntax.
⟨label⟩ :: = ⟨identifier⟩ | ⟨unsigned integer⟩
⟨switch identifier⟩ :: = ⟨identifier⟩
⟨switch designator⟩ :: = ⟨switch identifier⟩ [⟨subscript expression⟩]
⟨simple designational expression⟩ :: = ⟨label⟩|⟨switch designator⟩|
   (⟨designational expression⟩)
⟨designational expression⟩ :: = ⟨simple designational expression⟩|
   ⟨if clause⟩ ⟨simple designational expression⟩ **else** ⟨designational
   expression⟩

3.5.2. Examples. *17*

p9

Choose [*n* − *1*]

Town [**if** *y* < *0* **then** *N* **else** *N* + *1*]

if *A* *b* < *c* **then** *17* **else** *q* [**if** *w* ≦ *0* **then** *2* **else** *n*]

3.5.3. Semantics. A designational expression is a rule for obtaining a label of a statement (cf. section 4. Statements). Again the principle of the evaluation is entirely analogous to that of arithmetic expressions (section 3.3.3). In the general case the Boolean expressions of the if clauses will select a simple designational expression. If this is a label the desired result is already found. A switch designator refers to the corresponding switch declaration (cf. section 5.3. Switch declarations) and by the actual numerical value of its subscript expression selects one of the designational expressions listed in the switch declaration by counting these from left to right. Since the designational expression thus selected may again be a switch designator this evaluation is obviously a recursive process.

3.5.4. The subscript expression. The evaluation of the subscript expression is analogous to that of subscripted variables (cf. section 3.1.4.2). The value of a switch designator is defined only if the subscript expression assumes one of the positive values *1, 2, 3,* ..., *n*, where *n* is the number of entries in the switch list.

3.5.5. Unsigned integers as labels. Unsigned integers used as labels have the property that leading zeroes do not affect their meaning, e.g. *00217* denotes the same label as *217*.

4. Statements

The units of operation within the language are called statements. They will normally be executed consecutively as written. However, this sequence of operations may be broken by go to statements, which define their successor explicitly, and shortened by conditional statements, which may cause certain statements to be skipped.

In order to make it possible to define a specific dynamic succession, statements may be provided with labels.

Since sequences of statements may be grouped together into compound statements and blocks the definition of statement must necessarily be recursive. Also since declarations, described in section 5, enter fundamentally into the syntactic structure, the syntactic definition of statements must suppose declarations to be already defined.

4.1. Compound statements and blocks.

4.1.1. Syntax.

⟨unlabelled basic statement⟩ :: = ⟨assignment statement⟩ | ⟨go to statement⟩ | ⟨dummy statement⟩ | ⟨procedure statement⟩

⟨basic statement⟩ :: = ⟨unlabelled basic statement⟩ | ⟨label⟩ : ⟨basic statement⟩

⟨unconditional statement⟩ :: = ⟨basic statement⟩ | ⟨for statement⟩ | ⟨compound statement⟩ | ⟨block⟩

⟨statement⟩ :: = ⟨unconditional statement⟩ | ⟨conditional statement⟩

⟨compound tail⟩ :: = ⟨statement⟩ **end** | ⟨statement⟩ ; ⟨compound tail⟩

⟨block head⟩ :: = **begin** ⟨declaration⟩ | ⟨block head⟩ ; ⟨declaration⟩

⟨unlabelled compound⟩ :: = **begin** ⟨compound tail⟩

⟨unlabelled block⟩ :: = ⟨block head⟩ ; ⟨compound tail⟩

⟨compound statement⟩ :: = ⟨unlabelled compound⟩ | ⟨label⟩ : ⟨compound statement⟩

⟨block⟩ :: = ⟨unlabelled block⟩ | ⟨label⟩ : ⟨block⟩

This syntax may be illustrated as follows: Denoting arbitrary statements, declarations, and labels, by the letters S, D, and L, respectively, the basic syntactic units take the forms:

Compound statement:

    L: L:... **begin** S ; S ;...S; S **end**

Block:

    L: L:... **begin** D; D;.. D; S; S;...S; S **end**

It should be kept in mind that each of the statements S may again be a complete compound statement or block.

4.1.2. Examples. Basic statements:

    $a := p + q$

    go to *Naples*

    Start: *Continue*: W: $= 7.993$

Compound statement:

    begin $x := 0$; **for** $y := 1$ **step** 1 **until** n **do** $x := x + A[y]$;

        if $x > q$ **then go to** *STOP* **else if** $x > w - 2$ **then go to** S;

        Aw: *St*: $W := x + bob$ **end**

Block:

    Q: **begin integer** i, k; **real** w;

        for $i := 1$ **step** 1 **until** m **do**

            for $k := i + 1$ **step** 1 **until** m **do**

            begin $w := A[i, k]$;

                $A[i, k] := A[k, i]$;

                $A[k, i] := w$ **end** *for i and k*

    end *block Q*

4.1.3. Semantics.

Every block automatically introduces a new level of nomenclature. This is realized as follows: Any identifier occurring within the block may through a suitable declaration (cf. section 5. Declarations) be specified to be local to the block in question. This means (a) that the entity represented by this identifier inside the block has no existence outside it and (b) that any entity represented by this identifier outside the block is completely inaccessible inside the block.

Identifiers (except those representing labels) occurring within a block and not being declared to this block will be non-local to it, i.e. will represent the same entity inside the block and in the level immediately outside it. The exception to this rule is presented by labels, which are local to the block in which they occur.

Since a statement of a block may again itself be a block the concepts local and non-local to a block must be understood recursively. Thus an identifier, which is non-local to a block A, may or may not be non-local to the block B in which A is one statement.

4.2. Assignment statements

4.2.1. Syntax.
⟨left part⟩ :: = ⟨variable⟩ :=
⟨left part list⟩ :: = ⟨left part⟩ | ⟨left part list⟩ ⟨left part⟩
⟨assignment statement⟩ :: = ⟨left part list⟩ ⟨arithmetic expression⟩ |
  ⟨left part list⟩ ⟨Boolean expression⟩

4.2.2. Examples. $s := p[0] := n := n + 1 + s$
$$n := n + 1$$
$$A := B/C - v - q \times S$$
$$s[v, k + 2] := 3 - arctan(s \times zeta)$$
$$V := Q > Y \wedge Z$$

4.2.3. Semantics. Assignment statements serve for assigning the value of an expression to one or several variables. The process will in the general case be understood to take place in three steps as follows:

4.2.3.1. Any subscript expressions occurring in the left part variables are evaluated in sequence from left to right.

4.2.3.2. The expression of the statement is evaluated.

4.2.3.3. The value of the expression is assigned to all the left part variables, with any subscript expressions having values as evaluated in step 4.2.3.1.

4.2.4. Types. All variables of a left part list must be of the same declared type. If the variables are **Boolean** the expression must likewise be Boolean. If the variables are of type **real** or **integer** the expression must be arithmetic. If the type of the arithmetic expression differs from that of the variables, appropriate transfer functions are understood to be automatically invoked. For transfer from **real** to **integer** type the transfer function is understood to yield a result equivalent to
entier (E + 0.5)
where E is the value of the expression.

4.3. Go to statements

4.3.1. Syntax.
⟨go to statement⟩ :: = **go to** ⟨designational expression⟩

4.3.2. Examples.
go to 8
go to *exit* [n + 1]
go to *Town* [**if** y < 0 **then** N **else** N + 1]
go to if A b < c **then** 17 **else** q [**if** w < 0 **then** 2 **else** n]

4.3.3. Semantics. A go to statement interrupts the normal sequence of operations, defined by the write-up of statements, by defining its successor explicitly by the value of a designational expression. Thus the next statement to be executed will be the one having this value as its label.

4.3.4. Restriction. Since labels are inherently local, no go to statements can lead from outside into a block.

4.3.5. Go to an undefined switch designator. A go to statement is equivalent to a dummy statement if the designational expression is a switch designator whose value is undefined.

4.4. Dummy statements

4.4.1. Syntax.
⟨dummy statement⟩ :: = ⟨empty⟩

4.4.2. Examples.
  L:
  begin.... ; *John*: **end**

4.4.3. Semantics. A dummy statement executes no operation. It may serve to place a label.

4.5. Conditional statements

4.5.1. Syntax.
⟨if clause⟩ :: = **if** ⟨Boolean expression⟩ **then**
⟨unconditional statement⟩ :: = ⟨basic statement⟩ | ⟨for statement⟩ |
  ⟨compound statement⟩ | ⟨block⟩
⟨if statement⟩ :: = ⟨if clause⟩ ⟨unconditional statement⟩ |
  ⟨label⟩ : ⟨if statement⟩
⟨conditional statement⟩ :: = ⟨if statement⟩ | ⟨if statement⟩ **else**
  ⟨statement⟩

4.5.2. Examples. **if** $x > 0$ **then** $n := n + 1$
              if $v > u$ **then** V: $q := n + m$ **else go to** R
              if $s < 0 \vee P \leq Q$ **then** AA: **begin if** $q < v$ **then** $a := v/s$
                              else $y := 2 \times a$ **end else if** $v > s$ **then**
                              $a := v - q$
                              else if $v > s - 1$ **then go to** S

4.5.3. Semantics. Conditional statements cause certain statements to be executed or skipped depending on the running values of specified Boolean expressions.

4.5.3.1. If statement. The unconditional statement of an if statement will be executed if the Boolean expression of the if clause is true. Otherwise it will be skipped and the operation will be continued with the next statement.

4.5.3.2. Conditional statement. According to the syntax two different forms of conditional statements are possible. These may be illustrated as follows:

if B 1 **then** S 1 **else if** B 2 **then** S 2 **else** S 3; S 4

and

if B 1 **then** S 1 **else if** B 2 **then** S 2 **else if** B 3 **then** S 3; S 4

Here B 1 to B 3 are Boolean expressions, while S 1 to S 3 are unconditional statements. S 4 is the statement following the complete conditional statement.

The execution of a conditional statement may be described as follows: The Boolean expressions of the if clauses are evaluated one after the other in sequence from left to right until one yielding the value **true** is found. Then the unconditional statement following this Boolean is executed. Unless this statement defines its successor explicitly the next statement to be executed will be S 4, i.e. the statement following the complete conditional statement. Thus the effect of the delimiter **else** may be described by saying that it defines the successor of the statement it follows to be the statement following the complete conditional statement.

The construction

else ⟨unconditional statement⟩

is equivalent to

else if true then ⟨unconditional statement⟩

If none of the Boolean expressions of the if clauses is true, the effect of the whole conditional statement will be equivalent to that of a dummy statement.

For further explanation the following picture may be useful:

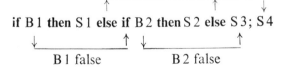

4.5.4. Go to into a conditional statement. The effect of a go to statement leading into a conditional statement follows directly from the above explanation of the effect of **else**.

4.6. For statements

4.6.1. Syntax.

⟨for list element⟩ :: = ⟨arithmetic expression⟩ |
  ⟨arithmetic expression⟩ **step** ⟨arithmetic expression⟩ **until**
  ⟨arithmetic expression⟩ |
  ⟨arithmetic expression⟩ **while** ⟨Boolean expression⟩
⟨for list⟩ :: = ⟨for list element⟩ | ⟨for list⟩, ⟨for list element⟩
⟨for clause⟩ :: = **for** ⟨variable⟩ : = ⟨for list⟩ **do**
⟨for statement⟩ :: = ⟨for clause⟩ ⟨statement⟩ |
  ⟨label⟩ : ⟨for statement⟩

4.6.2. Examples. **for** $q := 1$ **step** s **until** n **do** $A[q]:= B[q]$
  for $k := 1, V1 \times 2$ **while** $V1 < N$ **do**
  for $j := I + G, L, 1$ **step** 1 **until** $N, C + D$ **do**
  $A[k,j] := B[k,j]$

4.6.3. Semantics. A for clause causes the statement S which it precedes to be repeatedly executed zero or more times. In addition it performs a sequence of assignments to its controlled variable. The process may be visualized by means of the following picture:

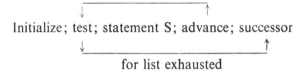

Initialize; test; statement S; advance; successor

for list exhausted

In this picture the word initialize means: perform the first assignment of the for clause. Advance means: perform the next assignment of the for clause. Test determines if the last assignment has been done. If so the execution continues with the successor of the for statement. If not the statement following the for clause is executed.

4.6.4. The for list elements. The for list gives a rule for obtaining the values which are consecutively assigned to the controlled variable. This sequence of values is obtained from the for list elements by taking these one by one in the order in which they are written. The sequence of values generated by each of the three species of for list elements and the corresponding execution of the statement S are given by the following rules:

4.6.4.1. Arithmetic expression. This element gives rise to one value, namely the value of the given arithmetic expression as calculated immediately before the corresponding execution of the statement S.

4.6.4.2. Step-until-element. An element of the form A **step** B **until** C, where A, B, and C, are arithmetic expressions, gives rise to an execution which may be described most concisely in terms of additional ALGOL statements as follows:

$$V := A;$$
$$L1: \textbf{if } (V - C) \times sign\,(B) > 0 \textbf{ then go to } \textit{Element exhausted};$$
$$\text{Statement S};$$
$$V := V + B;$$
$$\textbf{go to } L1;$$

where V is the controlled variable of the for clause and Element exhausted points to the evaluation according to the next element in the for list, or if the step-until-element is the last of the list, to the next statement in the program.

4.6.4.3. While-element. The execution governed by a for list element of the form E **while** F, where E is an arithmetic and F a Boolean expression, is most concisely described in terms of additional ALGOL statements as follows:

$$L3: \quad V := E;$$
$$\textbf{if } \neg \text{ F } \textbf{then go to } \textit{Element exhausted};$$
$$\text{Statement S};$$
$$\textbf{go to } L3;$$

where the notation is the same as in 4.6.4.2. above.

4.6.5. The value of the controlled variable upon exit. Upon exit out of the statement S (supposed to be compound) through a go to statement the value of the controlled variable will be the same as it was immediately preceding the execution of the go to statement.

If the exit is due to exhaustion of the for list, on the other hand, the value of the controlled variable is undefined after the exit.

4.6.6. Go to leading into a for statement.

The effect of a go to statement, outside a for statement, which refers to a label within the for statement, is undefined.

4.7. Procedure statements

4.7.1. Syntax.

⟨actual parameter⟩ :: = ⟨string⟩ | ⟨expression⟩ | ⟨array identifier⟩ |
⟨switch identifier⟩ | ⟨procedure identifier⟩
⟨letter string⟩ :: = ⟨letter⟩ | ⟨letter string⟩⟨letter⟩
⟨parameter delimiter⟩ :: = , |) ⟨letter string⟩ :(

⟨actual parameter list⟩ :: = ⟨actual parameter⟩ |
    ⟨actual parameter list⟩ ⟨parameter delimiter⟩ ⟨actual parameter⟩
⟨actual parameter part⟩ :: = ⟨empty⟩ | (⟨actual parameter list⟩)
⟨procedure statement⟩ :: = ⟨procedure identifier⟩ ⟨actual parameter
    part⟩

4.7.2. Examples. *Spur (A) Order: (7) Result to: (V)*
                  Transpose (W, v + 1)
                  Absmax (A, N, M, Yy, I, K)
                  Innerproduct (A[t, P, u], B [P], 10, P, Y)
These examples correspond to examples given in section 5.4.2.

4.7.3. Semantics. A procedure statement serves to invoke (call for) the
execution of a procedure body (cf. section 5.4. procedure declarations).
Where the procedure body is a statement written in ALGOL the effect
of this execution will be equivalent to the effect of performing the following operations on the program:

4.7.3.1. Value assignment (call by value). All formal parameters quoted
in the value part of the procedure declaration heading are assigned the
values (cf. section 2.8. Values and types) of the corresponding actual
parameters, these assignments being considered as being performed
explicitly before entering the procedure body. These formal parameters
will subsequently be treated as local to the procedure body.

4.7.3.2. Name replacement (call by name). Any formal parameter not
quoted in the value list is replaced, throughout the procedure body, by
the corresponding actual parameter, after enclosing this latter in parentheses wherever syntactically possible. Possible conflicts between
identifiers inserted through this process and other identifiers already
present within the procedure body will be avoided by suitable systematic
changes of the formal or local identifiers involved.

4.7.3.3. Body replacement and execution. Finally the procedure body,
modified as above, is inserted in place of the procedure statement and
executed.

4.7.4. Actual-formal correspondence. The correspondence between the
actual parameters of the procedure statement and the formal parameters of the procedure heading is established as follows: The actual
parameter list of the procedure statement must have the same number of
entries as the formal parameter list of the procedure declaration heading.

The correspondence is obtained by taking the entries of these two lists in the same order.

4.7.5. Restrictions. For a procedure statement to be defined it is evidently necessary that the operations on the procedure body defined in sections 4.7.3.1. and 4.7.3.2. lead to a correct ALGOL statement.

This poses the restriction on any procedure statement that the kind and type of each actual parameter be compatible with the kind and type of the corresponding formal parameter. Some important particular cases of this general rule are the following:

4.7.5.1. Strings cannot occur as actual parameters in procedure statements calling procedure declarations having ALGOL 60 statements as their bodies (cf. section 4.7.8).

4.7.5.2. A formal parameter which occurs as a left part variable in an assignment statement within the procedure body and which is not called by value can only correspond to an actual parameter which is a variable (special case of expression).

4.7.5.3. A formal parameter which is used within the procedure body as an array identifier can only correspond to an actual parameter which is an array identifier of an array of the same dimensions. In addition if the formal parameter is called by value the local array created during the call will have the same subscript bounds as the actual array.

4.7.5.4. A formal parameter which is called by value cannot in general correspond to a switch identifier or a procedure identifier, because these latter do not possess values (the exception is the procedure identifier of a procedure declaration which has an empty formal parameter part (cf. section 5.4.1) and which defines the value of a function designator (cf. section 5.4.4). This procedure identifier is in itself a complete expression).

4.7.5.5. Any formal parameter may have restrictions on the type of the corresponding actual parameter associated with it (these restrictions may, or may not, be given through specifications in the procedure heading). In the procedure statement such restrictions must evidently be observed.

4.7.6. Non-local quantities of the body. A procedure statement written outside the scope of any non-local quantity of the procedure body is undefined.

4.7.7. Parameter delimiters. All parameter delimiters are understood to be equivalent. No correspondence between the parameter delimiters used in a procedure statement and those used in the procedure heading is expected beyond their number being the same. Thus the information conveyed by using the elaborate ones is entirely optional.

4.7.8. Procedure body expressed in code. The restrictions imposed on a procedure statement calling a procedure having its body expressed in non-ALGOL code evidently can only be derived from the characteristics of the code used and the intent of the user and thus fall outside the scope of the reference language.

5. Declarations

Declarations serve to define certain properties of the identifiers of the program. A declaration for an identifier is valid for one block. Outside this block the particular identifier may be used for other purposes (cf. section 4.1.3).

Dynamically this implies the following: at the time of an entry into a block (through the **begin** since the labels inside are local and therefore inaccessible from outside) all identifiers declared for the block assume the significance implied by the nature of the declarations given. If these identifiers had already been defined by other declarations outside they are for the time being given a new significance. Identifiers which are not declared for the block, on the other hand, retain their old meaning.

At the time of an exit from a block (through **end**, or by a go to statement) all identifiers which are declared for the block lose their significance again.

A declaration may be marked with the additional declarator **own.** This has the following effect: upon a reentry into the block, the values of own quantities will be unchanged from their values at the last exit, while the values of declared variables which are not marked as own are undefined. Apart from labels and formal parameters of procedure declarations and with the possible exception of those for standard functions (cf. sections 3.2.4 and 3.2.5) all identifiers of a program must be declared. No identifier may be declared more than once in any one block head.

Syntax.

$\langle$declaration$\rangle$ :: = $\langle$type declaration$\rangle$ | $\langle$array declaration$\rangle$ |
$\qquad\qquad\qquad$ $\langle$switch declaration$\rangle$ | $\langle$procedure declaration$\rangle$

5.1. Type declarations

5.1.1. Syntax.
⟨type list⟩ :: = ⟨simple variable⟩ | ⟨simple variable⟩, ⟨type list⟩
⟨type⟩ :: = **real** | **integer** | **Boolean**
⟨local or own type⟩ :: = ⟨type⟩ | **own** ⟨type⟩
⟨type declaration⟩ :: = ⟨local or own type⟩ ⟨type list⟩

5.1.2. Examples. **integer** *p, q, s*
own Boolean *Acryl, n*

5.1.3. Semantics. Type declarations serve to declare certain identifiers to represent simple variables of a given type. Real declared variables may only assume positive or negative values including zero. Integer declared variables may only assume positive and negative integral values including zero. Boolean declared variables may only assume the values **true** and **false.**

In arithmetic expressions any position which can be occupied by a real declared variable may be occupied by an integer declared variable.

For the semantics of **own**, see the fourth paragraph of section 5 above.

5.2. Array declarations

5.2.1. Syntax.
⟨lower bound⟩ :: = ⟨arithmetic expression⟩
⟨upper bound⟩ :: = ⟨arithmetic expression⟩
⟨bound pair⟩ :: = ⟨lower bound⟩ : ⟨upper bound⟩
⟨bound pair list⟩ :: = ⟨bound pair⟩ | ⟨bound pair list⟩, ⟨bound pair⟩
⟨array segment⟩ :: = ⟨array identifier⟩ [⟨bound pair list⟩]|
⟨array identifier⟩, ⟨array segment⟩
⟨array list⟩ :: = ⟨array segment⟩ | ⟨array list⟩, ⟨array segment⟩
⟨array declaration⟩ :: = **array** ⟨array list⟩ |
⟨local or own type⟩ **array** ⟨array list⟩

5.2.2. Examples. **array** a, b, c [7:n, 2:m], s [− 2:10]
own integer array A [*if* $c < 0$ **then** 2 **else** 1: 20]
real array q [− 7: − 1]

5.2.3. Semantics. An array declaration declares one or several identifiers to represent multidimensional arrays of subscripted variables and gives the dimensions of the arrays, the bounds of the subscripts and the types of the variables.

5.2.3.1. Subscript bounds. The subscript bounds for any array are given in the first subscript bracket following the identifier of this array in the form of a bound pair list. Each item of this list gives the lower and upper bound of a subscript in the form of two arithmetic expressions separated by the delimiter: The bound pair list gives the bounds of all subscripts taken in order from left to right.

5.2.3.2. Dimensions. The dimensions are given as the number of entries in the bound pair lists

5.2.3.3. Types. All arrays declared in one declaration are of the same quoted type. If no type declarator is given the type **real** is understood.

5.2.4 Lower upper bound expressions.

5.2.4.1. The expressions will be evaluated in the same way as subscript expressions (cf. section 3.1.4.2).

5.2.4.2. The expressions can only depend on variables and procedures which are non-local to the block for which the array declaration is valid. Consequently in the outermost block of a program only array declarations with constant bounds may be declared.

5.2.4.3. An array is defined only when the values of all upper subscript bounds are not smaller than those of the corresponding lower bounds.

5.2.4.4. The expressions will be evaluated once at each entrance into the block.

5.2.5. The identity of subscripted variables. The identity of a sub-scripted variable is not related to the subscript bounds given in the array declaration. However, even if an array is declared **own** the values of the corresponding subscripted variables will, at any time, be defined only for those of these variables which have subscripts within the most recently calculated subscript bounds.

5.3. Switch declarations

5.3.1. Syntax.
$\langle$switch list$\rangle$ :: = $\langle$designational expression$\rangle$ |
    $\langle$switch list$\rangle$, $\langle$designational expression$\rangle$
$\langle$switch declaration$\rangle$ :: = **switch** $\langle$switch identifier$\rangle$: = $\langle$switch list$\rangle$

5.3.2. Examples. **switch** $S := S1, S2, Q[m]$ **if** $v > -5$ **then** $S3$ **else** $S4$
                          switch $Q := p1, w$

5.3.3. Semantics. A switch declaration defines the values corresponding to a switch identifier. These values are given one by one as the values of the designational expressions entered in the switch list. With each of these designational expressions there is associated a positive integer, $1, 2, \ldots$, obtained by counting the items in the list from left to right. The value of the switch designator corresponding to a given value of the subscript expression (cf. section 3.5. Designational expressions) is the value of the designational expression in the switch list having this given value as its associated integer.

5.3.4. Evaluation of expressions in the switch list. An expression in the switch list will be evaluated every time the item of the list in which the expression occurs is referred to, using the current values of all variables involved.

5.3.5. Influence of scopes. Any reference to the value of a switch designator from outside the scope of any quantity entering into the designational expression for this particular value is undefined.

   5.4. Procedure declarations

5.4.1. Syntax.
⟨formal parameter⟩ :: = ⟨identifier⟩
⟨formal parameter list⟩ :: = ⟨formal parameter⟩ |
   ⟨formal parameter list⟩ ⟨parameter delimiter⟩ ⟨formal parameter⟩
⟨formal parameter part⟩ :: = ⟨empty⟩ | (⟨formal parameter list⟩)
⟨identifier list⟩ :: = ⟨identifier⟩ | ⟨identifier list⟩, ⟨identifier⟩
⟨value part⟩ :: = **value** ⟨identifier list⟩; | ⟨empty⟩
⟨specifier⟩ :: = **string** | ⟨type⟩ | **array** | ⟨type⟩ **array** | **label** | **switch** |
   procedure | ⟨type⟩ **procedure**
⟨specification part⟩ :: = ⟨empty⟩ | ⟨specifier⟩ ⟨identifier list⟩; |
   ⟨specification part⟩ ⟨specifier⟩ ⟨identifier list⟩;
⟨procedure heading⟩ :: = ⟨procedure identifier⟩ ⟨formal parameter
   part⟩; ⟨value part⟩ ⟨specification part⟩
⟨procedure body⟩ :: = ⟨statement⟩ | ⟨code⟩
⟨procedure declaration⟩:: = **procedure** ⟨procedure heading⟩ ⟨procedure
   body⟩ | ⟨type⟩ **procedure** ⟨procedure heading⟩ ⟨procedure body⟩

5.4.2. Examples (see also the examples at the end of the report).
procedure *Spur* (*a*) *Order*: (*n*) *Result*: (*s*); **value** *n*;
array *a*; **integer** *n*; **real** *s*;
begin integer *k*;
s := *0*;

```
for k := 1 step 1 until n do s := s + a [k, k]
end
```

procedure *Transpose* (*a*) *Order:* (*n*); **value** *n*;
array *a*; **integer** *n*;
begin real *w*; **integer** *i, k*;
for *i* := *1* **step** *1* **until** *n* **do**
  for *k* := *1 + i* **step** *1* **until** *n* **do**
  begin *w* := *a* [*i, k*];
        a [*i, k*] := *a*[*k, i*];
        a [*k, i*] := *w*
  end
end *Transpose*
integer procedure *Step* (*u*); **real** *u*;
Step := **if** $0 \leq u \wedge u \leq 1$ **then** *1* **else** *0*

procedure *Absmax* (*a*) *size:* (*n, m*) *Result:* (*y*) *Subscripts*: (*i, k*);
comment *The absolute greatest element of the matrix a, of size n by m is transferred to y, and the subscripts of this element to i and k;*
array *a*; **integer** *n, m, i, k*; **real** *y*;
begin integer *p, q*;
y := *0*;
for *p* := *1* **step** *1* **until** *n* **do for** *q* := *1* **step** *1* **until** *m* **do**
if *abs* (*a*[*p, q*]) > *y* **then begin** *y* := *abs* (*a* [*p, q*]); *i* := *p*; *k* := *q* **end end**
  Absmax
procedure *Innerproduct* (*a, b*) *Order:* (*k, p*) *Result:* (*y*); **value** *k*;
integer *k, p*; **real** *y, a, b*;
begin real *s*;
s := *0*;
for *p* := *1* **step** *1* **until** *k* **do** *s*: = *s* + *a* × *b*;
y := *s*
end *Innerproduct*

5.4.3. Semantics. A procedure declaration serves to define the procedure associated with a procedure identifier. The principal constituent of a procedure declaration is a statement or a piece of code, the procedure body, which through the use of procedure statements and/or function designators may be activated from other parts of the block in the head of which the procedure declaration appears. Associated with the body is a heading, which specifies certain identifiers occurring within the body to represent formal parameters. Formal parameters in the procedure body will, whenever the procedure is activated (cf. section 3.2. Function designators and section 4.7. Procedure statements) be assigned the values of or replaced by actual parameters. Identifiers in the procedure body which are not formal will be either local or non-local to the body depending on whether they are declared within the body or not. Those of them which are non-local to the body may well be local to the block in the head of which the procedure declaration appears.

5.4.4. Values of function designators. For a procedure declaration to define the value of a function designator there must, within the procedure body, occur an assignment of a value to the procedure identifier, and in addition the type of this value must be declared through the appearance of a type declarator as the very first symbol of the procedure declaration.

Any other occurrence of the procedure identifier within the procedure body denotes activation of the procedure.

5.4.5. Specifications. In the heading a specification part, giving information about the kinds and types of the formal parameters by means of an obvious notation, may be included. In this part no formal parameter may occur more than once and formal parameters called by name (cf. section 4.7.3.2) may be omitted altogether.

5.4.6. Code as procedure body. It is understood that the procedure body may be expressed in non-ALGOL language. Since it is intended that the use of this feature should be entirely a question of hardware representation, no further rules concerning this code language can be given within the reference language.

Examples of procedure declarations

Example 1

procedure *euler* (*fct, sum, eps, tim*); **value** *eps, tim*; **integer** *tim*; **real**
procedure *fct*; **real** *sum, eps*;
comment *euler computes the sum of fct* (*i*) *for i from zero up to infinity by
means of a suitably refined euler transformation. The summation is stopped
as soon as tim times in succession the absolute value of the terms of the
transformed series are found to be less than eps. Hence, one should provide
a function fct with one integer argument, an upper bound eps, and an
integer tim. The output is the sum sum. euler is particularly efficient in
the case of a slowly convergent or divergent alternating series*;
begin integer *i, k, n, t*; **array** *m* [0:15]; **real** *mn, mp, ds*;
$i := n := t := 0; m[0] := fct(0); sum := m[0]/2;$
nextterm: $i := i + 1; mn := fct(i);$
$\quad\quad$ **for** $k := 0$ **step** *1* **until** *n* **do**
$\quad\quad\quad$ **begin** $mp := (mn + m[k])/2; m[k] := mn; mn := mp$
$\quad\quad\quad\quad$ **end** *means*;
$\quad\quad$ **if** $(abs(mn) < abs(m[n])) \land (n < 15)$ **then**
$\quad\quad\quad$ **begin** $ds := mn/2; n := n + 1; m[n] := mn$ **end** *accept*
$\quad\quad$ **else** $ds := mn;$
$\quad\quad sum := sum + ds;$
$\quad\quad$ **if** $abs(ds) < eps$ **then** $t := t + 1$ **else** $t := 0;$
$\quad\quad$ **if** $t < tim$ **then go to** *nextterm*
end *euler*

Example 2[1]

procedure *RK* (*x, y, n, FKT, eps, eta, xE, yE, fi*); **value** *x, y*; **integer** *n*;
Boolean *fi*; **real** *x, eps, eta, xE*; **array** *y, yE*; **procedure** *FKT*;

[1] This RK-program contains some new ideas which are related to ideas of S. GILL,
*A process for the step bp step integration of differential equations in an automatic
computing machine.* Proc. Camb. Phil. Soc. Vol. 47 (1951) p. 96, and E. FRÖBERG,
On the solution of ordinary differential equations with digital computing machines,
Fysiograf. Sällsk. Lund, Förhd. 20 Nr. 11 (1950) p. 136–152. It must be clear however that with respect to computing time and round-off errors it may not be optimal,
nor has it actually been tested on a computer.

comment: *RK integrates the system* $y_k = f_k(x, y_1, y_2, \ldots, y_n)$ $(k = 1, 2, \ldots n)$
*of differential equations with the method of Runge-Kutta with automatic
search for appropriate length of integration step. Parameters are: The
initial values x and y* [k] *for x and the unknown functions* $y_k(x)$. *The order
n of the system. The procedure* $FKT(x, y, n, z)$ *which represents the system
to be integrated, i.e. the set of functions* f_k. *The tolerance values eps and
eta which govern the accuracy of the numerical integration. The end of
the integration interval xE. The output parameter yE which represents
the solution at* $x = xE$. *The Boolean variable fi, which must always be
given the value* **true** *for an isolated or first entry into RK. If however the
functions y must be available at several meshpoints* $x_0, x_1, \ldots, x_n$, *then
the procedure must be called repeatedly (with* $x = x_k$, $xE = x_{k+1}$, *for* $k = 0$,
$1, \ldots, n-1$) *and then the later calls may occur with* $fi =$ **false** *which saves
computing time. The input parameters of FKT must be x, y, n, the output
parameter z represents the set of derivatives z* $[k] = f, (x, y[1], y[2], \ldots,$
$y[n])$ *for x and the actual y's. A procedure comp enters as a non-local identifier*;
begin
    array *z, y1, y2, y3* $[1:n]$; **real** *x1, x2, x3, H*; **Boolean** *out*;
    integer *k, j*; **own real** *s, Hs*;
    procedure *RK1ST* (x, y, h, xe, ye); **real** *x, h, xe*; **array** *y, ye*;
        comment: *RK1ST integrates one single Runge-Kutta step with initial
values x, y* [k] *which yields the output parameters* $xe = x + h$ *and
ye* [k], *the latter being the solution at xe.*
        Important: the parameters n, FKT, z enter RK1ST as non-local entities;
        begin
            array *w* $[1:n]$, *a* $[1:5]$; **integer** *k, j*;
            a $[1] := a[2] := a[5] := h/2; a[3] := a[4] := h; xe := x;$
            for $k := 1$ **step** 1 **until** n **do** *ye* $[k] := w[k] := y[k]$;
            for $j := 1$ **step** 1 **until** 4 **do**
                begin
                    FKT (xe, w, n, z);
                    $xe := x + a[j]$;
                    for $k := 1$ **step** 1 **until** m **do**
                    begin
                        w $[k] := y[k] + a[j] \times z[k]$;
                        ye $[k] := ye[k] + a[j+1] \times z[k]/3$
                  end *k*
            end *j*
        end *RK1ST*;

Begin of program:

  if *fi* **then begin** $H := xE - x; s := 0$ **end else** $H := Hs$;

  out := **false**;

AA: **if** $(x + 2.01 \times H - xE > 0) \equiv (H > 0)$ **then**

  begin $Hs := H$; *out* := **true**; $H := (xE - x)/2$ **end** *if*;

  $RK1ST(x, y, 2 \times H, x1, y1)$;

BB: $RK1ST(x, y, H, x2, y2); RK1ST(x2, y2, H, x3, y3)$;

  for $k := 1$ **step** 1 **until** n **do**

    if $comp(y1[k], y3[k], eta) > eps$ **then go to** CC;

  comment: *comp* (a, b, c) *is a function designator, the value of which is*
  the absolute value of the difference of the mantissae of a and b, after
  the exponents of these quantities have been made equal to the largest
  of the exponents of the originally given parameters a, b, c;

  $x := x3$; **if** *out* **then go to** DD;

  for $k := 1$ **step** 1 **until** n **do** $y[k] := y3[k]$;

  if $s = 5$ **then begin** $s := 0; H := 2 \times H$ **end** *if*;

  $s := s + 1$; **go to** AA;

CC: $H := 0.5 \times H$; *out* := **false**; $x1 := x2$;

  for $k := 1$ **step** 1 **until** n **do** $y1[k] := y2[k]$;

  go to BB;

DD: **for** $k := 1$ **step** 1 **until** n **do** $yE[k] := y3[k]$

end *RK*

Alphabetic index of definitions of concepts and syntactic units

All references are given through section numbers. The references are given in three groups:

def Following the abbreviation 'def' reference to the syntactic definition (if any) is given.

synt Following the abbreviation 'synt' references to the occurrences in metalinguistic formulae are given. References already quoted in the def-group are not repeated.

text Following the word 'text' the references to definitions given in the text are given.

The basic symbols represented by signs other than the words printed in bold face have been collected at the beginning. The examples have been ignored in compiling the index.

+ see: plus

− see: minus

× see: multiply

/ ÷ see: divide

↑ see: exponentiation

< ≤ = ≥ > ≠ see: ⟨relational operator⟩

≡ ⊃ ∧ ∨ ¬ see: ⟨logical operator⟩

, see: comma

. see: decimal point

$_{10}$ see: ten

: see: colon

; see: semicolon

:= see: colon equal

⊔ see: space

( ) see: parentheses

[ ] see: subscript bracket

' ' see: string quote

⟨actual parameter⟩, def 3.2.1, 4.7.1

⟨actual parameter list⟩, def 3.2.1, 4 7.1

⟨actual parameter part⟩, def 3.2.1, 4.7.1

⟨letter⟩, def 2.1 synt 2, 2.4.1, 3.2.1, 4.7.1
⟨letter string⟩, def 3.2.1, 4.7.1
local, text 4.1.3
⟨local or own type⟩, def 5.1.1 synt 5.2.1
⟨logical operator⟩, def 2.3 synt 3.4.5 text 3.4.5
⟨logical value⟩, def 2.2.2 synt 2, 3.4.1
⟨lower bound⟩, def 5.2.1 text 5.2.4
non-local, text 4.1.3
minus − , synt 2.3, 2.5.1, 3.3.1 text 3.3.4.1
multiply ×, synt 2.3, 3.3.1 text 3.3.4.1
⟨multiplying operator⟩, def 3.3.1
⟨number⟩, def 2.5.1 text 2.5.3, 2.5.4
⟨open string⟩, def 2.6.1
⟨operator⟩, def 2.3
own, synt 2.3, 5.1.1 text 5, 5.2.5
⟨parameter delimiter⟩, def 3.2.1, 4.7.1 synt 5.4.1 text 4.7.7
parentheses ( ), synt 2.3, 3.2.1, 3.3.1, 3.4.1, 3.5.1, 4.7.1, 5.4.1 text
    3.3.5.2
plus +, synt 2.3, 2.5.1, 3.3.1 text 3.3.4.1
⟨primary⟩, def 3.3.1
procedure, synt 2.3, 5.4.1
⟨procedure body⟩, def 5.4.1
⟨procedure declaration⟩, def 5.4.1 synt 5 text 5.4.3
⟨procedure heading⟩, def 5.4.1 text 5.4.3
⟨procedure identifier⟩, def 3.2.1 synt 3.2.1, 4.7.1, 5.4.1 text 4.7.5.4
⟨procedure statement⟩, def 4.7.1 synt 4.1.1. text 4.7.3
program, text 1
⟨proper string⟩, def 2.6.1
quantity, text 2.7
real, synt 2.3, 5.1.1 text 5.1.3
⟨relation⟩, def 3.4.1 text 3.4.5
⟨relational operator⟩, def 2.3, 3.4.1
scope, text 2.7
semicolon ; , synt 2.3, 4.1.1, 5.4.1
⟨separator⟩, def 2.3
⟨sequential operator⟩, def 2.3
⟨simple arithmetic expression⟩, def 3.3.1 text 3.3.3
⟨simple Boolean⟩, def 3.4.1
⟨simple designational expression⟩, def 3.5.1
⟨simple variable⟩, def 3.1.1 synt 5.1.1 text 2.4.3

space ⊔, synt 2.3 text 2.3, 2.6.3
⟨specification part⟩, def 5.4.1 text 5.4.5
⟨specificator⟩, def 2.3
⟨specifier⟩, def 5.4.1
standard function, text 3.2.4, 3.2.5
⟨statement⟩, def 4.1.1 synt 4.5.1, 4.6.1, 5.4.1 text 4 (complete section)
statement bracket see: **begin end**
step, synt 2.3, 4.6.1 text 4.6.4.2
string, synt 2.3, 5.4.1
⟨string⟩, def 2.6.1 synt 3.2.1, 4.7.1 text 2.6.3
string quotes ' ' , synt 2.3, 2.6.1 text 2.6.3
subscript, text 3.1.4.1
subscript bound, text 5.2.3.1
subscript brackets [ ], synt 2.3, 3.1.1, 3.5.1, 5.2.1
⟨subscripted variable⟩, def 3.1.1 text 3.1.4.1
⟨subscript expression⟩, def 3.1.1 synt 3.5.1
⟨subscript list⟩, def 3.1.1
successor, text 4
switch, synt 2.3, 5.3.1, 5.4.1
⟨switch declaration⟩, def 5.3.1 synt 5 text 5.3.3
⟨switch designator⟩, def 3.5.1 text 3.5.3
⟨switch identifier⟩, def 3.5.1 synt 3.2.1, 4.7.1, 5.3.1
⟨switch list⟩, def 5.3.1
⟨term⟩, def 3.3.1
ten $_{10}$, synt 2.3, 2.5.1
then, synt 2.3, 3.3.1, 4.5.1
transfer function, text 3.2.5
true, synt 2.2.2
⟨type⟩, def 5.1.1 synt 5.4.1 text 2.8
⟨type declaration⟩, def 5.1.1 synt 5 text 5.1.3
⟨type list⟩, def 5.1.1
⟨unconditional statement⟩, def 4.1.1, 4.5.1
⟨unlabelled basic statement⟩, def 4.1.1
⟨unlabelled block⟩, def 4.1.1
⟨unlabelled compound⟩, def 4.1.1
⟨unsigned integer⟩, def 2.5.1, 3.5.1
⟨unsigned number⟩, def 2.5.1 synt 3.3.1
until, synt 2.3, 4.6.1 text 4.6.4.2
⟨upper bound⟩, def 5.2.1 text 5.2.4
value, synt 2.3, 5.4.1